Contents

Publisher
Rick Bailey

Editorial Director
Theodore DiSante

Art Director
Don Burton

Book Design
Leslie Sinclair

Typography
Cindy Coatsworth,
Michelle Carter

Director of Manufacturing
Anthony B. Narducci

B&W Photos
Melchior DiGiacomo

Color Photos
Art Shay

Front Cover Photo
©Gregory Gorfkle, 1985.
All rights reserved.

Back Cover Photo
Courtesy of Pro-Kennex

Illustrations
Allan Mogel

Material prepared by
Rutledge Books, a division of
Sammis Publishing
Corporation, 122 E. 25th St.,
NY, NY 10010

Foreword

At the 1975 New England Pro-Am in South Burlington, Vermont, a revolution happened in the racquetball world. A brash, cocky, 17-year-old Marty Hogan suddenly burst out of obscurity onto the national racquetball scene. He beat three of the top four players on the professional tour to win his first pro racquetball tournament.

One player was Steve Keeley, runner-up in the 1973 IRA National Championships and frequent tour semifinalist. Another was Steve Serot, runner-up in two national championships, frequent tour finalist and heir-apparent to the then national champion, Charlie Brumfield, self-proclaimed greatest player of all time and winner of three national singles titles.

THE HOGAN GAME

Marty's sudden fame was indicative of his whole game at the time. He did everything in a big way. He hit balls with greater velocity than any player could imagine. He made mind-boggling shots that amazed everybody. It was the beginning of a new era—the Hogan era of the power game.

Up to this time the Hogan brand of racquetball was considered unorthodox, unenduring and definitely not something you would want to do or teach your kids. But after the Burlington tournament, tour players became more interested in the Hogan swing, the Hogan serve, and the Hogan strategy. Was it for real or would his arm fall off from the extended pendulum swing?

We know today, after Hogan's five national championships, that the pendulum swing is indeed correct and that a strategy could be forged with power as the major component. A new generation of players now emulates the Hogan technique. Marty Hogan was and is the most dominant player in the game of racquetball. No other player has revolutionized the game as much as he.

However, claiming that the Marty Hogan brand of racquetball is based solely on power is missing the evolution of both the Marty Hogan game and the game of racquetball itself. His style is at the heart of the modern game, which *has* changed. The equipment has changed. And so has Marty's approach to the game. He has learned much about strategy, tactics, shot-making and many other facets of the game since his early days. And it's all here! In this book you'll benefit from his years of experience and thrilling successes.

THE GAME AND BOOK FOR EVERYBODY

This book will benefit players at all levels, from beginner to advanced. Although Marty has directed his presentation to beginning and intermediate players, there is abundant material for advanced players too.

Beginners will find all of the fundamentals covered in a well-organized progression—from equipment to strategy. Advanced players find a discussion on advanced tactics and strategy. All players benefit from descriptions on efficient shot-making, the key to hitting the ball effortlessly with power, and all of the other facets of one of the fastest and most exciting games ever. Most important, Marty presents the material in straightforward, everyday terms that everyone can understand.

I also hope that you can benefit from some of my highlighted tips along the way. And don't ignore the 16 pages of color photos showing Marty and other pros in the thick of racquetball action.

Steve Garvey
San Diego, California

CHAPTER ONE

Racquetball In A Nutshell

Racquetball is a deceptively simple game everyone can enjoy—male and female, young and old. You can learn enough about the game in less than an hour to have a great time right away. You can also play it leisurely or at a fierce, competitive pace. Whether you are a klutz or super jock, you can have a great workout in about an hour. It's no wonder that my whole family plays racquetball for fun and exercise. Not only that, racquetball players are some of the nicest and most interesting people you will meet.

BASICS

Racquetball is normally played on an enclosed court 20 feet wide, 40 feet long, and 20 feet high. There are also other so-called official courts of the three-wall and one-wall variety, but I won't be talking about those.

The racquet is a small version of a tennis racket. With it you propel a small, hollow rubber ball toward the front wall. Essentially, the object is to return the ball to the front wall without letting it bounce on the floor more than once.

You can play *singles* (two players), *cut-throat* (three players), or *doubles* (four players). Most of this book discusses singles; chapter 20 is about doubles.

No special uniform is required. Most people wear ''court-style'' clothes when playing racquetball—shorts, an athletic shirt, and tennis shoes. If you play tennis, use your tennis clothes. If you are a student, a physical-education outfit works fine. Out of courtesy, it is customary for players to wear light-colored shirts so the dark ball can be clearly seen. Also, black-soled running shoes are discouraged because they will often mark the court floor.

Scoring—You can score a point only while serving, and you continue serving as long as you do not lose a *rally*, which is the play occurring after a serve. The first person—or team, in doubles—to earn 15 points wins the game. Two out of three games wins the match. The third game, if needed, is the *tie-breaker.* It is played to 11 points.

To win, a one-point margin is sufficient—15-14, 14-15, 11-10 would be an exciting *and* legal match score. Other match formats may be played in some tournaments. For example, a professional match is three out of five 11-point games.

The Serve—Play begins with the server in the *service zone* and the receiver in the *backcourt.* The server drops the ball and strikes it after one bounce so it hits the front wall first.

If the ball strikes any of the other walls, the floor, or the ceiling before hitting the front wall, the server loses the serve. If the ball hits the front wall first, it must then hit no more than one side wall before bouncing on the floor between the *short line* (the back line of the service zone) and the back wall.

If the ball hits two side walls or the back wall before landing on the floor, or if the ball hits the floor in front of the short line, the serve is a *fault.* The server then has one more chance to hit a legal serve. The server loses his serve after two service faults.

The Rally—The service returner must stand behind the *receiving line,* or *five-*

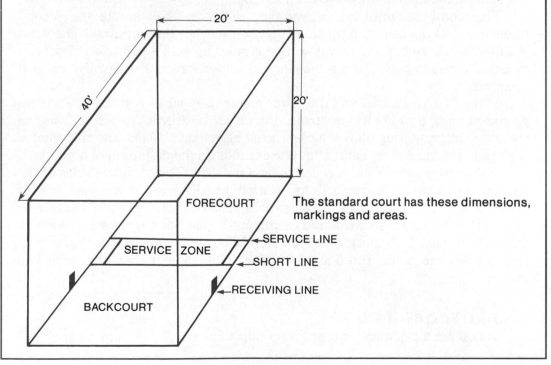

The standard court has these dimensions, markings and areas.

RECEIVING LINE

BACKCOURT

SHORT LINE

SERVICE ZONE

Here, play is about to begin. The server is in the service zone, and the receiver is in backcourt.

foot line, until the ball crosses it. Then he must hit the ball to return it to the front wall. He can bounce the ball off any of the walls or the ceiling after it bounces no more than once on the floor. He can even strike the ball before it bounces on the floor if he chooses.

Play continues until one player fails to hit the ball before the second bounce or hits the ball onto the floor before it reaches the front wall. The latter is called a *skip ball*. If the server wins the rally, he gets a point. If the service returner wins the rally, there is a change of server, called a *sideout*. No point is awarded.

If the ball you hit strikes the other player, play stops and the point is replayed because a *hinder* has occurred. If a player obstructs the path or view of the other player during play, the obstructed player calls *hinder,* and the point is replayed. The chapter on court etiquette expands on the definition of hinders.

These are the basics of racquetball in a nutshell. The complete rules of the American Amateur Racquetball Association (AARA) are at the back of this book. Be aware that the rules can change. Tournament players should subscribe to an official racquetball magazine or request a rule book from the AARA to keep up to date. This quick overview should be sufficient for any beginner to start playing the game. You'll learn the fine points in later chapters and as you play.

A WORD FOR BEGINNERS

If you are a beginner, you probably don't know a *Z ball* from a *ceiling ball,* or a *lob serve* from a *drive serve*. But you will. I've made a special effort to take you through the maze of terminology, shot-making techniques and strategies in a straightforward, easy-to-understand approach from the ground up. I think that you will be amazed at how fast you change from an inexperienced player to a good one.

I'm not expecting you to remember every little detail in our journey through this maze. But I'm hopeful that your game will mature to the point where you can experiment and learn on your own while using this book as an expert guide. It will teach you how to improve your game in a minimum amount of time by showing you what to practice and how to practice efficiently. Who knows? After you're armed with the knowledge in this book, maybe you'll become the racquetball guru at your local club.

A WORD FOR INTERMEDIATES

If you are an intermediate player, you're probably trying to get unstuck from a plateau. This book will help. It will give you a different perspective on the game and help you see the relationships between power and control and between strategy and shot-making. This book covers all of the modern strategies and shot-making techniques. I'm confident that you'll find worthwhile tactics, shots, or ploys to add to your game. From this different vantage point, you may be able to see more clearly how to step up to the next level of play.

A WORD FOR THE ADVANCED

If you are an advanced player, you've probably already discovered that there is more to the game of racquetball than meets the eye. The learning process is never over. Like life, the game is always changing. Ball design changes, requiring an adjustment to your strategy. Racquets change, offering you an opportunity to let technology add a few points to your game. Players change, presenting a stimulating mental and sometimes physical challenge for you to "figure out why he's beating me."

Among other things, this book will teach you the serve-and-shoot philosophy of racquetball. You can't really be an advanced player without knowing what it's about.

HOW TO READ THIS BOOK

The best way to use this book is to first read briskly through it entirely. Then start again from the beginning and cover each chapter more carefully. But don't think that you have to read the entire book before using the ideas on the court.

If you are a beginner, don't overlook the chapters on championship service strategy and shot-making. Even if you aren't an advanced player, those chapters will give you a peek into your potential future and provide motivation for practicing fundamentals.

If you are an advanced player, don't skip over the early chapters. They may improve your understanding of the game's basics. You will also want to read in depth those parts that cover your weak spots.

This way, you will discover new ideas in every chapter and perhaps even rediscover some old ideas when you find yourself in a racquetball rut. Whether you are a beginner or advanced player, you will be a better player because of this book and the Hogan power game.

By chapter 12, you will have the knowledge you need to play good racquetball, using basic shots and a fundamental strategy. The remainder of the book delves into greater degrees of sophistication that you can add to your basic shots and fundamental strategy. That part of the book deals with refinements of the fundamentals presented in the first part of the book.

You can still be a top-notch player even if you stick to the fundamentals and perfect only them. The refinements of the latter chapters are aspects of the advanced game that you can add to your game in small increments as you gain confidence and skill.

Racquetball is an exciting game. It's even more fun when you play it properly. I will teach you how to get the most out of the game in the shortest possible time. But pay attention and practice! There is something to be learned in every chapter.

At this point, an apology is in order before I offend the millions of left-handed and female players around the world who will also benefit from this book. Throughout, instructions are seemingly given for right-handed, male players. I think that if you are left-handed, you can make the mental and visual translation from my right-handed perspective to yours. Using male pronouns merely favors economy in words and does not imply any gender bias.

CHAPTER TWO

Equipment

Essential racquetball equipment is relatively inexpensive. Typically, you can get started with a small investment. In fact, if you already play some other court-type sport or run, you probably have most of the clothes you need. Basically, you should have nonrestrictive athletic shorts and appropriate underwear, a T-shirt, and athletic socks.

Specialized running shoes aren't designed for the quick starts, stops and turns of court sports, so don't use running shoes. Buy a pair of court or tennis shoes. I also recommend that you get sweatbands and protective eyewear.

Minimally, the only special equipment you will need is a ball and a racquet. Some clubs will rent or loan you a racquet. Balls are sometimes sold at clubs.

CHOOSING A RACQUET

The racquet is the most important piece of equipment because it's the link between you and the ball. Racquet technology has advanced much in the last few years. With a little effort, you can find the right model that complements your game.

Of course, I am partial to the racquets I have personally designed, but each player should try several racquets before choosing the one he plans to use. Following are the necessary things to consider when choosing a racquet:

Composition—Racquet materials have come a long way from the early days of heavy, wooden frames. Materials in use now include graphite, boron, fiberglass, nylon, aluminum, and steel. Each affects the various characteristics of control, power, and durability.

Control is a byproduct of a racquet that "holds" the ball on the strings a bit longer than usual. The racket flexes during impact with the ball and is considered *flexible*. Because control is enhanced at the sacrifice of some power, you can place shots.

A racquet is powerful if it efficiently transfers the force of your stroke into the ball and makes it move fast. Typically, power is related to a racquet's *stiffness*. The stiffer the racket, the better it transfers your force to the ball. Basically, aluminum, steel and 100%-graphite are stiff, giving you good power at the expense of some control. This makes a stiff racquet more unforgiving than a flexible one if you use an improper swing. A stiff racket can also transmit shock to your arm if you swing incorrectly. The result is usually a pain in the elbow called *tennis elbow*.

Traditionally, control and power were opposites—you sacrificed one to get the other in a particular racquet. Some modern, "high-tech" materials have changed that. Materials such as graphite, boron and a variety of composites offer just the right combination of flexibility *and* stiffness, thus giving you both control and power in one racquet.

This discussion may make racquet selection seem difficult. But it doesn't have to be. There's a simple solution: In most cases, choice is a matter of your personal game and budget.

Here's why: Racquet technology is so advanced now that in most cases, you don't have to worry about a bad buy. For most players, the technical mumbo-jumbo of composition isn't critical. What is important is how the racquet feels to you. Don't worry if a friend is using a $200 racquet if you find a $30 racquet that feels great.

Price vs. Performance—Be sure to match your budget and ability with the racquet. A $100 racquet is not necessarily twice as good as a $50 racquet. But if you plan to pay a high price for a racquet, be assured that you won't be wasting your money. Spending $100 or more will buy you the best that technology can offer.

High-priced racquets offer every advantage that you can get from technology alone. The racquet probably wouldn't break even if you tried to break it. With it you can quickly alternate between blasting a ball crosscourt and tapping a soft drop shot into the corner, both with control.

One big difference between less expensive and more expensive racquets is durability. Aluminum, fiberglass and fiberglass/nylon racquets, which typically populate the lower price ranges, usually deform or break after a year or two of heavy use—or abuse, such as hitting the wall. Racquets using nylon may also warp at high temperatures, such as when they are stored exposed to summer heat. Of course, if you are careful, they may last longer. You may also find that some durable, low-priced racquets are heavy. This is because such designs use more material for greater strength.

Every year, racquet manufacturers produce more exotic racquets. It's tough—and expensive—to keep up with the state-of-the-art. If you care about high-tech specs, consult a magazine that has an annual racquet review.

Pro-Kennex and I have teamed up to produce six different racquets. The Blaster Series, shown here, and the Marty Hogan Performance Series feature various compositions of graphite, aluminum alloys, and fiberglass for different types of players. Other racquet manufacturers also produce more than one type of racquet. With a little effort you can find the racquet that complements your game.

Even so, you can't avoid the fact that the racquet that *feels* best will help you *play* your best. It can be a confusing mixture of personal taste and how you swing: Do you want to hit the ball as fast as possible all of the time? Do you have a tendency to get tennis elbow? Do you like a control game? Are you "all wrist"? The list of questions can go on and on.

Grip Size—This is the perimeter of the grip, typically measured in inches. In racquetball, the right size grip lets you put good *wrist snap* into your shots. Wrist snap is an important element in power and control. I and most players find that the right grip size for a racquetball racquet is smaller than the right grip size for a tennis racket. I use a 3-7/8 inch and 4-1/2 inch grip, respectively, for those two sports.

If in doubt about what grip size is best for you, ask a knowledgeable salesperson or go with the smaller grip. A small grip is easy to enlarge, but a large grip usually can't be reduced.

Weight—A light racquet requires you to use relatively more wrist than arm stroke to power the ball. A heavy racquet is better for blocking balls or punching shots. Typically, high-tech materials like graphite or graphite/boron composite are light yet very durable.

Tournament players typically use racquets that are about 230 to 250 grams (8 ounces). If you are a beginner, you might want to start with a slightly heavier racquet. But if the racquet is much heavier, it may limit your ability to execute strokes properly.

If you play tennis or squash, a heavier racquet may feel best at the outset. As your game improves you will probably prefer a lighter racquet.

Strings and String Tension—So-called *gut* strings—which are widely used in tennis rackets—offer no advantage over nylon in racquetball racquets. If you are having a racquetball racquet restrung, get a good multifilament nylon string for best overall results. In my experience, the normal stringing pattern is best.

Typical string tensions range from 25 pounds to 32 pounds, but you should consult your local stringing shop for advice on the recommended tension for your racquet. If necessary, write to the racquet manufacturer.

Basically, the greater the tension, the more power per shot and the less control. But again, personal taste and abilities are important here. Some players like mushy strings at 18 pounds or tight ones at 35 pounds.

Trial Racquet—Try a racquet before you buy it. For example, find a friend who has the same kind of racquet that you are thinking of buying. Using it will help you decide whether to buy one or not.

In addition, some sporting-goods stores will rent racquets and then apply your rental fee to the purchase price of the racquet. Others have loaner racquets that you can use for a few days.

Adjustment Period—It may take a few sessions to get used to a racquet if you already play racquetball and are switching to a different racquet. Be patient. Eventually you'll adapt to the characteristics of the new racquet.

Guarantee—Don't buy any racquet that has a warranty period of 30 days or less. It won't be a good deal over the life of the racquet. No matter what racquet you buy, be sure to mail in the guarantee card.

As You Change—As you and your game change, perhaps from timid defense to aggressive offense, so may your racquet needs. But the racquet won't change your game dramatically. Only practice and dedication will. At best a different racquet, properly chosen, will help you maximize your skills by complementing your style of play. Because every player is different, the right racquet is different from player to player.

OTHER EQUIPMENT

All of the following equipment is essential. Whether you play infrequently or many times a week, you'll need this stuff.

Racquetballs—You'll find a variety of ball manufacturers, colors, and degrees of *liveliness*. If you're a beginner, consider using a slow ball. This way you can get accustomed to the game before using a livelier ball. I know of some players who prefer using an old, dead ball to make their rallies last longer. Playing with a zippy ball is no fun if your opponent can hit it much harder than you can.

If you have some racquetball experience, don't worry too much about ball selection. Use the brand that your club or friends provide. Basically, you should use the ball that makes the game fun.

However, as you get better and start playing tournaments, you should find out what the official ball is. You will probably discover that there are at least two or three brands of "official" balls. Use the official ball for the next tournament you plan to enter or the ball that seems most popular.

Eyewear—Racquetball is officially a noncontact sport. Even so, the ball sometimes makes contact with a player. To be safe, wear athletic eyewear to protect you from a stray ball that may hit you in the eyes. Many racquetball facilities say that you *must* wear eye protection while playing. Furthermore, proper eyewear will give you confidence when watching the ball. Confidence is essential for good anticipation and to know when to give your opponent more room to swing.

If you normally wear glasses while playing, look into getting shatterproof lenses and athletic-quality frames that are strong enough to protect your eyes and pliable enough to be comfortable.

For maximum safety, use athletic eyewear that covers the eyes. However, if you have trouble with excess perspiration on your lenses, try lensless ones. I use an eye guard with lenses that you can find in any sporting-goods store or pro shop.

Sweatbands—In my opinion, wristbands are a must. As you begin to perspire, the sweat trickles down your arm and onto your racquet grip. A wristband will absorb enough of the flow so that intermittent towelings during breaks will keep the racquet grip from getting soaked.

Using the right equipment promises safe and fun racquetball. I'm wearing non-regulation dark clothing in this book so you can "read" the how-to photos clearly. I wouldn't wear clothes this dark in a match.

If you play racquetball a lot, a duffel bag is handy. These have a lot of room and separate compartments for racquets, clothes and damp items.

Headbands are necessary to keep sweat out of your eyes and off your glasses. In addition, less sweat will splash around the court and long hair will stay under control.

Glove—A glove helps keep the grip surface dry, reducing the chance of slippage. Less slippage means a greater transfer of power from the racquet to the ball.

Gloves can be expensive but don't have to be. They can be as much as $12 for a fine sheepskin type or as little as $1.25 for a cotton liner from a handball glove.

Some players refuse to use a glove because they say that it reduces their "feel" of the racquet. Instead, they use a minitowel to keep their hands dry. A minitowel is a handtowel tucked under the waistband of your shorts. Between each point or as the need arises, wipe the grip and your hands with the towel. When the towel gets wet, replace it with a dry one.

CHAPTER THREE

Court Etiquette

Who wants to play the crowder, the cheater, the blocker, or the griper? Nobody does. Everyone wants a game with a player who gives ample room to swing, offers an unobstructed path to the ball, and projects a positive, friendly attitude when playing. Good court etiquette makes racquetball fun and safe.

There are both written and unwritten rules of etiquette. In tournament play, a referee is on hand to enforce the written rules. However, in club play there is no referee, and you are obligated only by social pressure and your conscience to adhere to the written rules of etiquette. Be assured that if you never follow any of the unwritten rules, no one will phone you for a game.

THE WRITTEN RULES

You'll find official rules of the game at the back of this book, so I won't list them here. However, there is an elementary rule of court etiquette that can't be overstressed.

Hinder—It states that a player is entitled to a fair chance to see and return the ball. This means that it is the responsibility of the player who has just hit the ball to move in a direction giving the other player an unobstructed approach and enough room to take a full swing. If this is not possible, the obstructed player can call *hinder,* forcing the point to be played over.

If you have hit the ball, you don't have to make a mad dash for the opposite wall. Use common sense. Take a circular route that gives the other player ample room, yet keeps you properly positioned on the court. For example, if you hit the ball along the near side wall, move forward one step, then away from the side wall one or two steps, and then finally back into position after the other player has had a chance to move through your original court position.

In tournament play, if a player deliberately obstructs the other player, the referee will call an *avoidable hinder* and the offending player automatically loses the rally. For example, if it is obvious that your opponent is about to hit the ball down along the side wall, you must not move into the lane along the side wall to block the flight of the ball to the front wall.

Avoidable hinders are almost never called during social play. People who use avoidable-hinder tactics to gain an advantage just don't get asked to play.

But the rules have to be interpreted rationally. For example, if a player hits a surprise serve that normally could be seen by the returner but the returner looks in the wrong direction, the situation does not warrant a hinder call.

Or, suppose a player hits a shot straight back at his body so the returner can't see the ball. If it is impossible to retrieve because the returner is out of position or falls down, this is not a hinder.

It should also be obvious that you can't distract, scream or stomp your feet when the other player is preparing to return the ball. The guiding rule is that each player must get a fair chance at striking the ball when it is his turn.

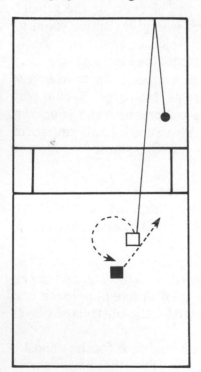

Note: In this and subsequent drawings, the open square represents the person who has just hit the ball; the solid square represents the defender. A dashed line typically indicates footwork by a player. A solid line shows ball motion, with the ball being the solid circle.

After you hit the ball, you must give your opponent a fair chance to see and return it. Your opponent has the right of way. If you get in his way, you've hindered. If the hinder was intentional, you've lost the rally.

THE UNWRITTEN RULES

Apply the Golden Rule in every situation. Unwritten rules call for honesty, courtesy, respect for your opponent, and a sense of fair play.

Playing Room—You might ask, "How much of a hitting lane should I give the other player?" In tournaments, players constantly tread the line on this point by giving the other player as little room as possible without the referee calling an avoidable hinder. A defending player will often give the other player the lane along the nearer side wall but will partially block the crosscourt lane.

In social play, it's better to give your opponent enough room so that he can hit the ball to any part of the front wall. You would probably be more than satisfied if your opponent were to give you that much freedom on every shot.

Hit by the Ball—If you hit the other player with the ball, either because you lost control of the shot or he was a little slow moving out of the way, it's best to apologize and give the hit player a chance to recover his wits. Getting hit can hurt! Then play the point over.

Unsure Calls—If you are not sure whether a ball skipped or whether you hit the ball before it bounced twice on the floor, offer to replay the point. But don't stop play if you are unsure about the call. It is better to continue playing a point and then ponder the situation *after* the rally is finished. You won't get much exercise if you stop play every few seconds.

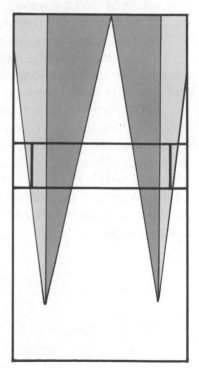

The four areas highlighted are considered *scoring lanes.* Typically, most winning shots are made in these zones. There's a lot of action there, so try to keep the lanes unobstructed.

If you stop play with a call, be certain of your decision. It may be best for you and your opponent to make some arrangement before the game. For example, some players prefer to play out all questionable calls. Some rely on the receiving player to make calls.

Stalling—Don't stall. It is OK to take a few seconds to catch your breath even when the other player is ready. But you shouldn't be milling around the court looking at the scenery after every rally when the other player is ready. When you need a little extra time, call a time-out.

In an informal game, rest when both of you want to. In competition, there is a rule that says the ball must be served within 10 seconds after the referee calls out the score. This was instituted to prevent long stalls and delays. In the days before the 10-second rule, some tournament matches would last for several hours. Similar matches today last for about an hour.

Officially, there are a limited number of short time-outs that can be called in each game. In a pickup game, though, these rules are normally relaxed.

Attitude—If you are being clobbered either because you are outclassed or are having a bad day, don't give up. Keep trying and be as competitive as you can. Simplify your strategy and shot selection so you can concentrate on basics. You might get a second wind—physically and mentally.

When on the court, you should at least get some exercise. If you just quit, you won't be doing yourself any good. You will have wasted the other player's time and inhibited your improvement. Losing is a part of the game because you will learn more by playing better players.

Projecting a positive attitude with lots of hustle will make the game more pleasant for all. In the long run, it will pay off in an improvement in your game and an ability to play through rough times.

Unfortunately, some tournament play will feature players who will not follow *any* of the unwritten rules. They take every advantage of the written ones. I'll cover such situations in later chapters when I discuss tournament play in more detail.

Summary—If you follow the written and unwritten rules, you will spend many happy hours on a racquetball court and have plenty of worthy opponents. If not, no one will want to play you. And then you won't be able to use what you learn from this book.

CHAPTER FOUR

Warmup, Conditioning And Diet

Having a positive mental attitude will certainly help you get the most out of racquetball, and so will good physical preparation. A proper warmup, the right duration and intensity of play, a good diet, and healthful rest are inextricably related to good athletic performance. Every player should be conditioned for his level of play—the higher the level, the more physically demanding the game.

WARMUP

When you are 15 years old, you always feel like you can hit the ball super fast, and you probably can. When you are 40, you may feel like you can hit the ball just as fast, but because you are much more susceptible to injury there's a danger in doing so. This is why you must warm up before you play hard. An improper warmup, or none at all, can lead to sore muscles, a sore elbow, and even severe injury. You can't get much out of racquetball if you are always aching. In fact, a good warmup is so important that even a 15-year-old player should do it.

Why and When—The idea is to increase the blood flow through your muscles before you start pushing them to their limit. You don't have to do much. Just five or ten minutes of light calisthenics and stretching before you get on the court will be sufficient for a beginner. When you get on the court, jog around it a few times. An advanced player may want to spend more time stretching before getting on the court.

Stretching—Attain a full stretch using slow motions. Then hold the fully stretched position for about a minute. If you feel pain, you are stretching too far. Do not bounce or use quick, jerky motions because these can have counter-productive effects and sometimes cause small muscle tears.

Warm up your arms by moving them slowly in a wide, circular motion. This exercise is sometimes called the *windmill*. Bend over and touch your toes to loosen up the back and the back of your legs. If you have recently turned your ankle or have weak ankles, rotate your foot slowly for a while. Bounce lightly on the balls of your feet for a minute to loosen lower leg muscles. There are many other exercises you could do, depending on your disposition and inclination, but these exercises will get you started.

On-the-Court Warmup—When you get on the court and finish the brief jog, begin by hitting the first few balls softly. Drop the ball and hit it once. Let the ball return to you, and repeat the process. Don't try to hit a series of shots, one right after the other without a break. Concentrate on increasing the range of your swing in small amounts until you can achieve full arm extension.

Then try over-accentuated arm movement to stretch your joints and muscles—not to hit the ball with maximum power. Begin with simple shots and progress through the range of shots in your repertoire—forehand, backhand, overhead, etc.

Opponent Warmup—I have observed that most racquetball players do not warm up by hitting the ball back and forth to each other. If this includes you, change your habits! It is an excellent way to warm up, work on your strokes, and also learn a bit about your opponent's game.

Of course, this type of warmup is possible only if both players are willing to cooperate. Begin by agreeing that each player will stay on his half of the court. Start slowly and hit the ball across the court to each other in a V pattern, back and forth. If you mishit the ball straight back to your own side, gently tap the ball across the court to your partner so that he can get a chance to hit the ball. After you have worked on the crosscourt shot to one side, switch sides and warm up the other crosscourt shot.

Don't get too fancy. Concentrate on watching the ball and swinging smoothly. Relax your mind and try to establish the appropriate awareness and attitude for the upcoming match.

Clothes—If the air is chilly, wear a warmup suit or sweat clothes when you go through the exercises and during the first few minutes on the court.

AMOUNT OF PLAY

The duration and intensity of play will be governed by your fitness and abilities. Beginners who hardly ever exercise will find that they will be exhausted after only 15 to 30 minutes of rigorous play. Advanced players may feel little physical exertion in a similar time period. Each time you play, you should improve cardiovascular stamina. The end result will make you a better, healthier player.

Frequent Player—An ardent beginner should play three or four times a week for about an hour each time. Basically, the amount of play each time should be enough to push yourself *slightly* beyond the level of fatigue.

Anything more can be counterproductive because you will be too tired to make proper strokes. In addition, you risk elbow, shoulder or some other injury. Anything less will not exercise your body enough to have one day's conditioning carry over to the next session. Consequently, your conditioning will improve very slowly. If you can force yourself to reach the right fatigue point, your stamina will increase dramatically in a few weeks.

Steve Garvey on Stretching

A good warmup not only helps you avoid injury. It is also the best way to insure that you can deliver maximum performance and gain maximum benefits from the exercise. I use almost the same stretching exercises for racquetball as I use before a baseball game. Stretching is particularly important when I've had a tough baseball game the day before because my muscles are tight and susceptible to tears. The brief warmup allows me to enjoy injury-free baseball *and* racquetball.

Weekend Player—If you don't play three or four times per week, but only on weekends, you can still improve stamina by doing other types of exercise. Running, swimming, bicycling, and jumping rope are four other activities that improve conditioning.

Advanced Players—If this includes you, you may find that three or four one-hour sessions per week will not be enough to significantly improve conditioning. To maintain a high level of play, quickness, flexibility, strength, and endurance must be maintained or improved.

Typically, three to four one-and-a-half hour sessions per week will do the job. Use the time wisely. One of the differences between the intermediate and the advanced player is that the latter knows how to use his time better. He plays with greater purpose and intensity during his workouts than the intermediate player.

Supplement general play at the advanced level with specific exercises and drills. The irony of being a good player is that the better you get, the less you have to run because you control shots better and make the other guy do all the work. Racquetball at the advanced level requires explosive speed with start-and-stop running. Playing other sports requiring this type of running helps develop physical skills that carry over to racquetball and can make training less monotonous.

For example, I have played squash, tennis, and basketball as a change of pace. Running short sprints, back and forth in a relay fashion, with adequate breaks, is a good supplement for developing quickness. One drill is to run along the inside perimeter of a court, picking up balls placed in the four corners of the court. This exercise requires running low and bending down, two skills required for good kill shots. Distance running is good for developing endurance, but will not help your quickness.

FOOD FOR FITNESS

Even if it goes without saying, I'll say it anyway: The right diet is one that keeps you healthy and energetic. For some people, a change in diet can produce dramatic improvements. In this context the word *diet* means the food you eat, not a calorie-reducing regimen.

Too many people eat excessive amounts of sugar, salt, and fatty foods. These people will be more sluggish and out of shape than those eating correctly. Athletes who have substantially reduced daily sugar intake have found a new level of energy they never thought they could attain. Fatty foods tend to stay in the stomach far longer than vegetables or potatoes, creating a long-lasting feeling of fullness.

I'm not a believer in special diets, although there are those who religiously follow various "health" diets. Special diets are often invented and then discredited. However, many still have large followings. Perhaps some have merits, but you have to be careful and know what you are doing before strictly following a special diet supplemented with vigorous racquetball.

Basic Principles—My family has always stressed the simple balanced diet that you are usually taught in grade school. In my experience, if you eat a balanced meal with items chosen from the four basic food groups, you should get plenty of nutrition to play racquetball without using vitamin supplements.

The four basic food groups and some examples from each are:

1) Milk group: milk, cheese, yogurt.

2) Protein group: meat, fish, poultry, eggs, beans, nuts.

3) Fruit and vegetable group: apples, bananas, oranges, tomatoes, spinach, broccoli, cabbage.

4) Cereal and grain group: rice, whole-wheat bread, oatmeal, sunflower seeds.

Of course, the quantity of food you should eat will depend on the amount of exercise you do. Try to get two servings each day from groups 1 and 2 and four servings from 3 and 4.

If your diet doesn't come close to a balanced meal from the four basic food groups, you should seriously think about changing your habits. But don't try to do it overnight. Sudden, drastic dietary changes may cause more damage than good because of the psychological and physiological shock of the change. Change your diet slowly. Let your body—and mind—get a chance to get used to the new habits.

Eating for Competition—There is always a great debate about when and what you should eat before playing. There is no consensus, merely some trends. Most top players do not eat during the two-hour period prior to a match. Typically, what they do eat at the meal before the match are foods such as spaghetti, pancakes, and whole-wheat bread.

Here's why: Complex carbohydrates such as macaroni and whole-grain products usually digest in less than two hours. The food is quickly converted to energy, in time for the upcoming competition. Protein-rich, fatty foods, such as beef, digest more slowly and won't provide a lot of energy in time.

Complex carbohydrates are mostly in food groups 3 and 4. Basically, they are sugars and starches that come from plants. White sugar (sucrose) is the worst substance for quick energy because it shocks the body with instant energy and a subsequent letdown, while supplying no other nutrients.

Water—Perhaps the most overlooked nutrient is water—before, during and after a match. Some players drink a lot of water a couple of hours before a match. This helps prepare them for the workout ahead.

During a vigorous match, you can lose two to four quarts of water. If this water is not replaced, both energy and endurance are decreased because muscles won't function at their maximum. Drink water during appropriate breaks in the match. Don't supplement the water with anything. It is a misconception that you should take salt or potassium tablets during a long, hot match to replace lost sodium or potassium ions. Although they are essential for proper muscle functioning, you get enough ions in regular, balanced meals.

I once knew some players who lost their matches terribly after following their local racquetball guru's suggestion that eating a lot of bananas *just before* a match would prevent muscle cramps. Bananas do contain a relatively high concentration of potassium, but enough water consumed during the matches would have prevented any cramps unless the players were out of shape.

After a vigorous match, drink water until your thirst is satisfied. Don't drink until you feel bloated.

CHAPTER FIVE

Centercourt Strategy

Essentially, racquetball is a simple game with a simple strategy: The key to winning is the *centercourt strategy*. Champions at all levels of play build their game around it. Unlike shot-making, which can sometimes go sour, centercourt strategy serves as a base for consistent, aggressive play.

When your offense refuses to fire up, centercourt strategy can carry you until your shots begin to score again. When your shots are working, centercourt strategy helps in applying constant pressure to your opponent. Centercourt strategy is also a method that lets you expend as little energy as possible while getting many scoring opportunities.

THE CENTERCOURT

The term *centercourt* is somewhat of a misnomer because it doesn't really mean the exact center of the court. Instead, the "playing" center is about five feet behind the short line and equidistant from the side walls. The area is a bit indefinite, but for the sake of discussion and practice, consider the area defined by the radius equal to a big step plus a stretch from the center.

Why There?—The player who can consistently occupy centercourt usually wins—for three very good reasons:

1) Simple geometry applies here. Almost all imperfect shots travel through centercourt. Carefully watch a match, and you will notice that even top players can't always keep their shots out of centercourt. Because we don't make perfect shots all of the time, centercourt is the hub around which each rally moves. It is

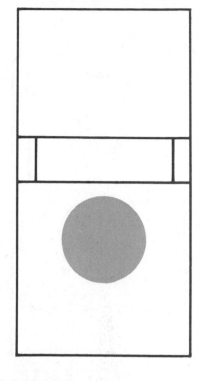

Centercourt is the shaded area shown here. It's the place to be to get the winning edge.

where you can capitalize on every mistake your opponent makes.

2) At centercourt you have maximum scoring options from effective shots. You can hit along the wall, across the court, or into the corner with equal ease and deception and still remain in position for your next shot. If you are off to the side of the court, and you mishit, you will probably be hopelessly out of position for the next shot.

3) You can cover your opponent's best shots with equal ease from centercourt. It takes only two or three steps to get to any spot where a good shot might be played. With good anticipation, you should be able to reach every shot except for a *rollout*—a shot that doesn't bounce but rolls after hitting low on the front wall.

When to Give It Up—Although centercourt is the most cherished location on the court during a rally, there are times when you must relinquish it. The rules say that you must *always* give up your position—centercourt or not—to give the other player a fair chance to hit the ball.

Beginners often misunderstand the centercourt strategy and refuse to move from centercourt even when they are hindering play. For safety's sake and to obey the rules, each player must always be aware of where the other player and the ball are. Move out of centercourt when the situation dictates.

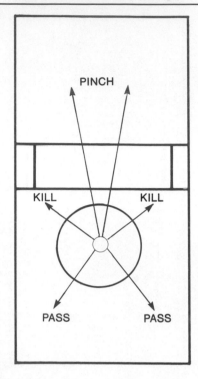

From centercourt you can cover most shots with equal ease. These and other shots are described and shown later.

Remember, you don't own centercourt. You must earn the right to occupy it through good play.

When to Take It—In a well-played match, each player drives the other player out of centercourt with, for example, a crosscourt shot. Players jockey back and forth, waiting for an offensive opportunity from a mishit.

If one player angles his shot too much or not enough, the ball will come through centercourt. When this happens, the centercourt player has a better position, with the other player trapped behind or near a side wall, and a scoring opportunity.

The proper action is to try to score with a kill shot that hits low on the front wall and travels away from the other player. If successful, the centercourt player ends the point. If not, the centercourt player may get a chance to score on a weak return. Or the jockeying continues again, with each player trying to take and stay in centercourt.

The next time you hear someone say, "He really controlled the center," you'll know that player used centercourt strategy. Anyone who doesn't use it is severely handicapped. By the end of the first game, the centercourt player will be fresh, while his unknowledgeable opponent will be huffing and puffing his way to a losing match.

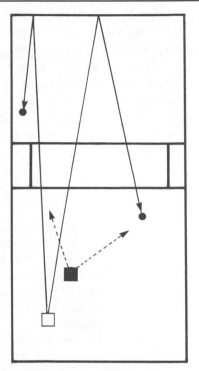

This example shows two ways to regain centercourt. With either shot, the defender must leave centercourt to return the ball. That opens centercourt for the other player.

COURT COVERAGE

To take full advantage of the centercourt position, you should adjust your spot on the court relative to the situation and anticipate the next shot. It doesn't take very long to learn to read shots and seemingly cover the entire court.

The basic rule to follow is that you should position yourself to cover those shots that the other player is most likely to make. Then move from that position only after your opponent can no longer change his shot. Following are some situations illustrating what I mean:

Situation 1a—Suppose that your opponent is in the left-rear corner and the ball comes to his backhand. If he hasn't shown you his favorite shot from this spot, dare him to hit across the court to your forehand by standing to the left and behind the center spot. Be far enough to the left of centercourt to tempt him to hit to your forehand, but not enough to hinder him or take you out of position.

As he begins his swing, watch the position of his feet and the motion of his shoulders to see if he intends to hit cross court or along the left wall. As his racquet starts its downswing, begin to move forward and toward the side of the expected return. By now, he has committed to one shot and cannot change his shot effectively. Your forward motion will carry you into the return.

One of the biggest mistakes made by beginners is that they play too close to the front wall. Beginners have less reason to move close to the front wall than an advanced player because beginners' opponents usually don't have enough offensive shots to warrant moving close to the front wall.

Never wait for a return while standing in front of the short line. If you play too close to the front wall, you will find yourself either constantly running to the backcourt to retrieve passing shots or find yourself jammed by medium-high balls. By starting from a deeper position in the backcourt—close to centercourt—you can see if the return will jam you and avoid it by curtailing forward advance early.

Steve Garvey on Centercourt

I tend to run around the ball to hit a forehand when the ball comes straight from the front wall through centercourt. This works well for me because I consider the forehand my strongest shot. But occasionally I stray too far into the backhand side to make the shot and get burned. This happens when I can't react fast enough to a ball coming at me from the side wall. If I can remember to stay in centercourt, away from the side walls, I get a lot more setups.

However, if you find that your opponent's pet shot is a crosscourt screamer that is hard to handle, you'll have to move your center spot to the right but still in deep backcourt. You can often neutralize a power shot by staying farther back in the court because a hard-hit ball will carry deeper into the backcourt. There really isn't any need to stand way up front. Furthermore, by playing deeper and making your first move forward, you will be able to translate forward momentum into greater power in your next shot.

Advanced players often position themselves deep in the backcourt and then "flow" into the play as the ball is struck. Playing in deep court gives them a better view of their opponent and allows them to watch the entire play develop. They respond to every piece of information they see.

Imagine yourself in the advanced player's shoes. You read your opponent's body language. Your brain processes the signals ever faster as your opponent's swing moves toward the point of contact with the ball—a time when it is perfectly clear what the ensuing shot will be.

Meanwhile, you make small adjustments in response to what you see. You lean forward in anticipation of a good shot. You start to take a step forward and to your left as your opponent's downswing begins. At the last moment you see an early pivot of your opponent's hips, indicating a crosscourt shot. Your feet respond quickly, shifting directions to the right but still moving forward. The ball leaves your opponent's racquet strings. Even though the ball is traveling

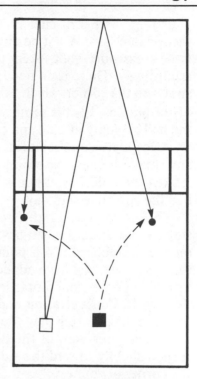

This is how an advanced player might "flow" into two shots if he is in backcourt.

crosscourt, you're already half way to where you should be. You meet the ball near midcourt and stroke the ball firmly along the right wall for a winner, leaving your opponent perplexed by your dazzling speed.

Situation 1b—The ball is in the backcourt as in Situation 1a, except this time you see that your opponent has barely had enough time to prepare for the return shot. You see immediately that he will definitely hit a weak shot along the left wall. Your weight should be on the balls of your feet in preparation for a quick movement.

But this time, there's no need to move forward with the downswing. Instead, you wait and as the ball is released from the strings, you make a quick decision. Will the ball be low enough for you to step forward and cut it off with a return shot or should you take it off the back wall?

If it's high, position yourself to take the ball off the back wall. If your opponent is trapped in the backcourt, hit the ball low into the left corner. If he rushes the forecourt, hit the ball down the wall.

Situation 2a—You have just hit the ball into the right forecourt, and your opponent is sprinting toward the ball from backcourt. You see that he will barely reach the ball.

In this situation, hold your position at centercourt. Most likely, he will hit the ball hard crosscourt. As he begins his swing, put your weight on the balls of your feet. As his racquet makes contact with the ball, you must make a split-second decision: Will it be anything except the anticipated crosscourt shot? If it is a crosscourt shot, step to the left and cut off the ball. If not, adjust accordingly. There is no need to move forward unless your opponent taps a soft shot into the corner, which he probably can't do anyway at a full gallop.

Situation 2b—It's the same situation as 2a, but this time your opponent gets to the ball in plenty of time and can hit the ball almost anywhere.

Don't give up. Look for any clues as to what he will do. If he doesn't offer any, make a guess based on what he has done in the past. Then move as he strikes the ball. If you guess wrong, you really haven't lost much because he had the advantage anyway.

But if you guess right, he will be out of position in forecourt, and you can step in and drive the ball past him for a winner. You've now won both a point on the scoreboard and a point psychologically. If he didn't botch his shot this time, you will still have added pressure to the next similar situation. He won't be able to forget your fantastic return!

Footwork, Concentration and Experience—These are but a few of the variables that can arise during play. But in all situations footwork is important. You can maximize your view of the developing play if you stagger your feet so you are turned slightly toward the side of the court with the ball. Watch the ball out of the corner of your eye.

To take full advantage of centercourt position, you must adjust your spot in the centercourt area. You learn it only by practice and watching other players. As you improve from rank beginner to a competitive player, you will notice a continuity developing. Instead of always bumping into your opponent, you will learn to flow in and out of centercourt with fewer breaks in the rhythm of the action.

CENTERCOURT DRILL

This simple drill will help you with the court movement demanded by centercourt strategy. First find a willing partner. He doesn't have to be at your level. Second, don't take your racquets, just a ball. Third, mark the centercourt spot with some tape.

Beginning—Start with one player holding the ball while standing on the marked spot and the other player in backcourt. The player with the ball throws it to the front wall high enough for it to rebound into a backcourt corner.

The other player retrieves the ball and throws the ball in a crosscourt pattern and runs toward the center spot while the other player moves out of centercourt. Continue doing this back and forth for a few minutes. You can choose the rapidity of the exchange to match your mastery of the movement.

Action Gallery

Transparent court walls allow for a large gallery. The effect of an excited crowd on players definitely influences the quality of play.

Is Charlie Brumfield hindering Hogan? It depends on where the ball is going.

Here, Brumfield is starting to move toward his next shot. Anticipation and quick reflexes are critical.

Shannon Wright is in centercourt, trying to keep Lynn Adams out of it.

In vigorous match play, perfect form is not always possible. Even so, try to stay with the basics, such as the wrist snap in this example.

Here, Bret Harnett is touching the wall during a backhand windup. This way, he isn't distracted by the wall during the shot. He senses its nearness with his hands.

Hillecher and Bledsoe keeping their eyes on the ball.

Marty Hogan's concentrated follow-through.

Variations—After you are comfortable with the centercourt pattern, try different patterns such as up and down one wall, deep balls, shallow balls, balls through the middle. Eventually use an unpredictable pattern produced by each player choosing a direction and height that makes the other player run far.

You can vary the rules to suit your own needs. For example, at first, allow the ball to take as many bounces on the floor as you like. Then restrict the maximum number to, say, three or four. Keep decreasing the maximum allotted number of bounces until you get down to the one allowed in a legal rally.

You will find that there are about 10 basic movement patterns that will occur. Some of these are shown below.

This drill will teach you how to move with minimum interference, making the game more enjoyable and intensifying the rallies. Soon, you too will feel that there is enough room to move freely, flowing in and out of centercourt.

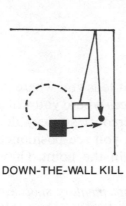

DOWN-THE-WALL KILL

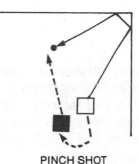

PINCH SHOT

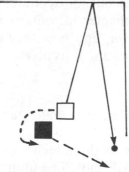

DOWN-THE-WALL DRIVE

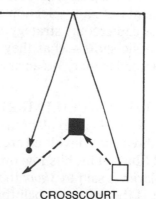

CROSSCOURT

With each of the four offensive shots shown, the player who just hit the ball moves toward centercourt when his opponent goes after the ball. Selecting the right shot makes it easier to win. It's the subject of the next chapter, too.

CHAPTER SIX

Shot-Selection Strategy

Centercourt strategy is a simple idea that works. It tells you where you can expect action to be concentrated and therefore the places where you will get the greatest number of scoring opportunities. But centercourt strategy does not necessarily tell you which shot you should take once you are positioned well. Nor does it tell you which shots will most likely win the point. Only shot-selection strategy does that.

The *kill/pass/ceiling* rule and the principle of *complementary shots* are basic elements of shot-selection strategy. These two simple but indispensable ideas make centercourt strategy almost unbeatable. This chapter introduces you to the basic shots—what they are, what they are used for, and how they can be combined to give you an arsenal that is greater than the sum of its parts.

KILL/PASS/CEILING RULE

Before I can explain the principles of the rule, you need to understand what the three shots involved are all about.

Kill Shot—This hits low on the front wall—about two or three inches or lower. A player is said to *shoot* the ball when he tries for a kill shot. The ultimate kill shot is the *rollout*—a ball that hits so low that it rolls from the front wall and is therefore unplayable.

A kill shot is the ultimate offensive weapon. It can be hit straight into the front wall or into a front corner. A kill shot traveling with tremendous velocity

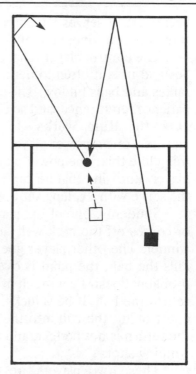

This is an example of when you should go for a kill. If you can intercept the ball in the service zone with your opponent out of position, try a pinch shot to the left side. Remember, make a kill shot if you get the chance.

is very demoralizing because there is absolutely no chance to touch the ball, let alone return it.

There is an element of risk in attempting a kill shot—a slight error can mean a skip ball and a lost rally. Many hours of practice are necessary to develop the timing required to hit an effective kill.

Passing Shot—Also called a *drive,* the passing shot hits higher on the front wall than a kill shot but usually with enough velocity so it literally passes by your opponent. It is normally a defensive weapon, but it can also be used offensively when the situation permits. Effective passing shots are hit directly to the front wall and can travel either along one of the side walls or in a V pattern across the court.

Passing shots are typically used to draw the opposition out of centercourt. The problem with passing shots is that they tend to reach the back wall before bouncing twice on the floor and therefore give the alert player a chance to turn the tables on you. Passing shots have a large margin for error—a shot a few degrees off is OK. It is the favorite shot of the quick player who can run all day. He uses it to win by tiring his opponent.

Ceiling Shot—It is purely a defensive shot hit into the ceiling about two to five feet from the front wall. It rebounds from the ceiling onto the front wall and finally down to the floor where it rebounds again into a high arc toward backcourt. It serves much the same purpose as the defensive lob does in tennis. It moves your opponent out of centercourt and into the backcourt.

The control player relishes the slower pace that accompanies ceiling-ball rallies and uses it often to neutralize the power shooter who prefers quick, frantic rallies and balls hit low. The perfect ceiling-ball rally reduces the game to one of patience, endurance, and selective shooting rather than speed and strength.

How the Rule Works—In a tightly contested match between two skilled players—one a power player, the other a control player—rallies resemble something like this: The power player blasts a serve to the control player. The control player, knowing that he can't match the power player in raw firepower, returns the serve with a ceiling shot. A ceiling-ball rally ensues.

Suddenly, one of the players mishits a ceiling shot and the ball drops short or comes off the back wall slowly. This is a *setup,* a shot that is easy to hit for a winner. The other player goes on the offensive and moves in for the kill. If he kills the ball, the point is over. If he nearly kills the ball, the defending player probably doesn't get much of a choice. He's forced to use any means possible to return the ball. If he is lucky, he will be able to drive the ball to the back of the court or hit the ball into the ceiling to give himself time to recover. Typically, the return is not perfect, and the offensive player gets another chance to make a winning shot.

These two players are both following the kill/pass/ceiling rule of shot selection: Kill if you get the chance; if you can't make a kill shot, try for a passing shot; make a ceiling shot only as a last resort.

At first it may seem that everybody would select the same predictable shots if they used this rule. But in actuality this is not so. Each player will have a different response because of perceived ability to hit an effective shot in each situation. For example, the power player thinks that any ball below the waist is an offensive opportunity. The control player is a bit more skeptical. Such differences make shot selection an exciting and unpredictable part of the game.

In spite of how you perceive your abilities, there are situations in which you *must* attempt a kill shot, no matter what kind of player you are. For example, suppose you are in centercourt and your opponent is behind you. Or, you are behind your opponent, but he's off to the side of the court. In either case, centercourt strategy and the kill/pass/ceiling rule dictate that you try a kill shot. Having scoring opportunities does you no good if you don't take advantage of them. Even if you don't win the point with an outright kill shot, you may get another chance on a weak return from your opponent.

Furthermore, you will have given notice to your opponent that he can never expect a free ride, and that you intend to attack him with aggressive shot selection every chance you get. In the long run, the pressure brought to bear by such a philosophy will lead to more errors from your opponent.

The alternative is to hit a passing shot, sending your opponent on the run to the back of the court. Although you have not lost the point, you may not have gained one either. If he should get to the passing shot, he could hit a lucky winner or neutralize your advantage by moving you from centercourt. In either case, you've lost an offensive opportunity and prolonged the rally more than necessary.

Some players contend that the kill shot is risky because a slight error can result in a skip ball—a ball that hits the floor before reaching the front wall. Theoretically, this is true. But in practice, kill attempts sometimes turn into passing shots. Passing shots seldom turn into kill shots!

Steve Garvey on the Ceiling Shot

The ceiling shot was the most revolutionary shot for me. I was excited to learn about it because it meant that I could get out of trouble by hitting up into the ceiling. And, the ceiling shot didn't even have to be great to work. For a while none of my friends knew how to deal with it. But as they learned to return it, I learned to hit a better one.

I try to aim for a spot on the ceiling about two or three feet from the front wall. I don't worry about hitting it too hard because most players have trouble with the ceiling shot coming off the back wall. But they're getting used to the hard ceiling, so I may have to be a little more careful. I also hit my ceiling shot close to the middle of the court to avoid hitting the side walls. The ceiling shot lets me play a more relaxed game because I know it's always there if I need it.

If your opponent is way out of position, raise the front-wall target slightly to insure a greater margin for error and therefore reduce the risk of a skip. Furthermore, how will you ever learn to score under pressure if you don't exploit offensive opportunities? You must learn by trying—and sometimes failing.

However, you can't go for a kill shot on every ball. If you don't have time to get ready for your shot or are out of position, try instead to hit a passing shot. Passing shots are normally used to return waist-high shots that you get while you are on the run. A good one moves your opponent from centercourt and opens it up for you.

If the situation is so difficult that you can't even hit a passing shot, hit a ceiling shot. For example, any ball over your head or at your ankles when you are in a fully stretched position should be returned with a ceiling shot. It gives you time to regain control and get back in the rally.

One bleak situation that dictates a kill shot instead of a defensive, ceiling shot is when you are on the run and there's a choice between hitting a halfhearted lob or hitting a winner to end a long rally. In this case, it's better to put the whole point on the line by trying a kill shot. If you miss and hit a skip ball, the point is over and you haven't wasted breath on what was a losing situation anyway.

If you adhere to the kill/pass/ceiling rule, you will develop a positive, disciplined frame of mind. This translates into a more aggressive style of play. The result elevates your game much faster than using a rule based on grinding out every point.

COMPLEMENTARY SHOTS

A boxer with a big right cross doesn't have to be feared if that's all he has. Every time he uses it, you can see it coming and duck. The skilled boxer has a variety of punches and sets his opponent up with a few jabs, a shot to the body, and then the big punch. The same holds for racquetball shots.

Racquetball shots come in pairs—each shot the complement of the other. Having one shot without its complement makes the shot less effective. Having an array of complementary shots diversifies your attack and reduces your opponent's ability to correctly anticipate your shots. This forces him to cover more of the court than you have to.

Using Coverage Zones—The court can be divided into four zones, as shown in the accompanying illustration. Each zone is the same size. A *coverage zone* is the quadrant a player has to run to when retrieving the ball.

One shot complements another if the two shots create coverage zones lying along a diagonal of the court. For example, shots that force a player to move from the left forecourt to the right backcourt are complementary. So are shots that move the player from the right forecourt to the left backcourt.

Obviously, complementary shots reduce the anticipation and control your opponent can exercise. They force him to change court position often—and run the longest distance to retrieve the shots you make. For example, the forehand, down-the-wall and pinch shots are complementary because their coverage zones are the right-rear and left-front corner, respectively. The forehand *down-the-wall* shot will hit the front wall and travel parallel to the right wall on its way to backcourt. The *pinch* is a kill shot that hits a front corner—side wall first. A forehand *near-side pinch* in this case would hit the right wall first, then the front wall.

When you get a setup on your forehand, hit your forehand kill so the shot parallels the wall on your forehand side. When your opponent starts to favor the right side and leans too early, hit a near-side pinch shot—in this case into the right corner—with him trapped in the backcourt.

Alternatively, hit a near-side pinch shot until he moves up to cover it. Then smash the ball by him along the right wall. With these two shots in your

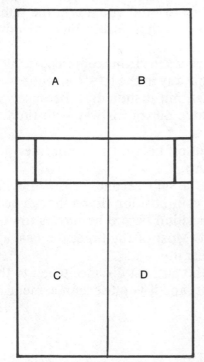

Areas labeled A, B, C and D are called *coverage zones.*

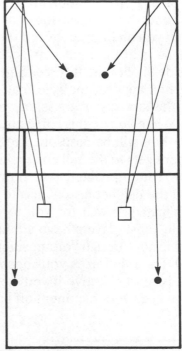

The down-the-wall and near-side pinch shots are complementary because they must be covered in zones A and D or zones B and C.

repertoire, your opponent can't anticipate what shot you are hitting unless you telegraph it through your swing. Many hours spent practicing the down-the-wall and the pinch, while using almost the same swing, promises improved deception.

Because the near-side pinch shot is a sure loser if it is hit too high, beginners should favor the down-the-wall kill on a forehand setup from centercourt. Use the pinch shot to keep your opponent guessing.

Conversely, the near-side pinch shot is a better pointmaker than the down-the-wall kill because of the angle and the distance from centercourt presented to the other player. Advanced players normally elect to hit a sharp, pinch shot on forehand setups from centercourt. They use the down-the-wall shot to keep their opponent honest.

Shot Selection—Much depends on your opponent's court location. It certainly doesn't make sense to hit a pinch shot if he is in forecourt. When selecting an offensive shot, choose one that keeps your current court location between your opponent's position and the coverage zone of the shot.

For example, if your opponent is in centercourt and you are in the right-front zone, hit a down-the-wall kill shot. Such a shot forces him to move through you on his way toward the right wall.

If he is in the right-rear zone and you have a shot from centercourt, hit a near-side pinch shot. It forces him past you on his way to the left-front zone.

When applied, the rule may cause a hinder, but it shouldn't. Because you know the strategy of the shot, you should move out of his way with time to spare. When you do this correctly, there are three effects:

1) You will be positioned to step in and cut off his return just in case your opponent gets to the ball and makes a good return.

2) Your opponent will normally hesitate a split second before moving toward the ball because he has to run through your position. Even though he is not obligated to wait for you to vacate your position before he moves toward the ball, most players have a tendency to wait. Most of the time, the best approach is not through your position, but only near it.

3) The rule forces your opponent to run the farthest distance to get to the ball. It is most effective if you are in centercourt and if you use complementary shots to keep your opponent off balance.

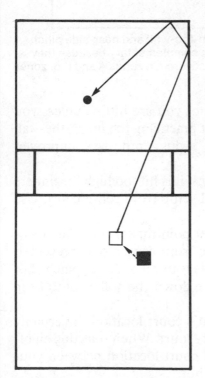

Perhaps the easiest strategy to remember is to hit a shot that forces your opponent to run through your position.

Everything I've said about the forehand down-the-line and pinch shots also applies for the backhand side. Learning these two shots on the backhand side is even more important because players tend to attack the backhand and stay away from hitting to the forehand.

OTHER GOOD SHOTS

Although the down-the-wall and the near-side pinch shots are fine complementary shots, you should have others. Consider these when you aren't holding on to centercourt.

When you are in backcourt, the *V-ball,* or *deep-crosscourt,* shot can move your opponent out of centercourt. Then you can assume that position and make a follow-up complementary shot or kill.

However, this strategy does have some pitfalls. Because the ball you hit has such a long distance to travel, the shot is susceptible to being cut off at the middle of the court by a fast, alert opponent. Remember, he is at centercourt, giving him a good chance at the majority of shots you make.

This situation is more likely to happen when your crosscourt shot ends up on his forehand side, rather than his backhand side. Usually, the crosscourt to the backhand side makes it safely to the rear because most players can't prepare themselves and release a backhand shot as fast as a forehand. Even if the crosscourt is cut off with a quick backhand slap, you will have a full view of the situation and can adjust your coverage accordingly.

Another point to consider is that a down-the-wall shot spends much less time in the air than a crosscourt shot, giving your opponent less time to react. One reasonable strategy is to go with the high-percentage shots: Hit a crosscourt shot from the back of the right-rear zone to the backhand side. Make a down-the-wall shot from the back of the left-rear zone to the backhand side. If you are a right-hander playing a left-hander, switch the shots in these conditions.

Beginners have a tough time controlling the down-the-wall shot. It leaves less margin for error. If it is too close to the side wall, it will hit it and rebound into the center of the court. If it is too far from the side wall, it gets close to the center of the court. At worst, you've given your opponent a setup that will end the point. At best, the rally continues and you are still out of centercourt.

In a mismatch, the less-experienced player spends his time watching the game from the backcourt because he can't execute crosscourt shots well enough to get control of centercourt. Therefore, the proper starting point for the beginner is first the crosscourt drive and then the down-the-wall drive. The beginner must have the shots that help capture centercourt before he can use the down-the-wall kill or pinch.

CHAPTER SEVEN

The Forehand

I have started with the forehand because it is the easiest basic shot to learn. Perhaps this is because many of us have participated in other activities, such as baseball or tennis, requiring similar arm motions. It's also good to start here because when you learn the mechanics of the forehand, you will be able to hit many of the standard serves.

This chapter begins with the fundamentals of hitting the forehand drive from a setup. I describe the elements forming an ideal forehand, starting with the proper grip and progressing through the different phases of the stroke. Also included is the role of the wrist snap and the pendulum swing in generating power. Then I describe how to hit the kill shot, ending with drills that will help you improve your forehand.

A big forehand is always an asset. Some top professional players depend almost exclusively on their big forehand for scoring. These swift players "run around" their backhand, always looking for the chance to hit a forehand winner. They are fast enough to cover the wide-open forehand side of the court.

The player with the big forehand is sometimes difficult to play. He conceals many of his shots because he can hold back on the forehand much longer than the backhand and still be effective. He uses unfamiliar shot patterns, which are hard to read until you've seen them many times. And he presents a very narrow backhand lane, making it difficult for you to concentrate your attack on his backhand.

FOREHAND GRIP

Forehand grips are variations of three classic tennis grips—Western, Eastern, and Continental. I can't overemphasize the importance of starting with a proper grip. The grip lets you "feel" your shots.

The grip you learn as a beginner will probably stay with you for the rest of your racquetball life. Once you develop the feel, you will have to go through a long adjustment period if you decide to make a drastic grip change. Therefore, you should learn the correct grip now. Any frustration will be well worth the effort.

Western Grip—The Western grip should never be used in racquetball. Basically, the palm of the hand rests on the lower right side of the grip when the racquet head is perpendicular to the floor. Unfortunately, beginners tend to try this grip—perhaps because it is a natural baseball bat type of grip. But this grip robs the forehand of power and makes it extremely difficult to switch to the backhand grip during quick exchanges.

Eastern Grip—Many players use the Eastern grip. The palm rests on the right side of the grip when the racquet head is perpendicular to the floor. This is a good forehand grip for those who can't adapt to a modified Continental grip. If you use this grip, you should use the *two-grip system,* in which you change to a different grip for the backhand. It is fairly easy to change from the Eastern forehand grip to the backhand grip during a quick exchange.

Continental Grip—In the Continental grip, the palm rests on the top of the grip. Some players use this grip for their backhand when the Eastern grip is used for the forehand.

This illustration shows where your palm rests for different grips, as described above.

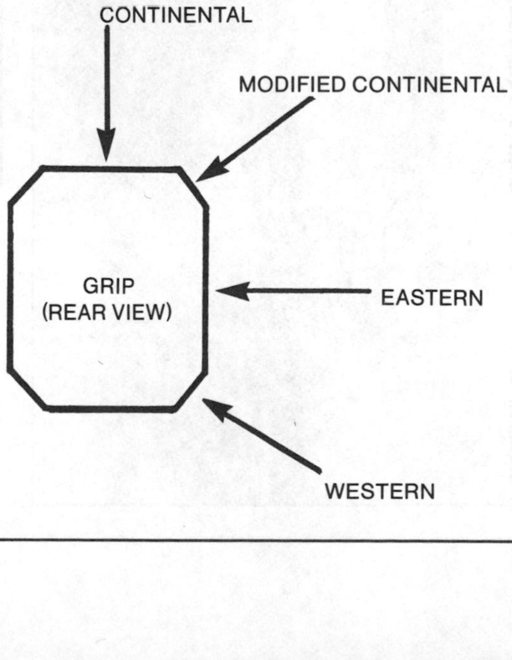

CONTINENTAL

MODIFIED CONTINENTAL

GRIP
(REAR VIEW)

EASTERN

WESTERN

I use a *modified* Continental grip in which the palm rests midway between the Eastern and Continental grip positions. The modified Continental grip is extremely versatile because you can use it for both backhand and forehand shots. This *one-grip system* minimizes grip-change errors during fast-paced rallies. I can keep my hand firmly on the racquet instead of having to loosen it and turn the racket during play. However, the one-grip system requires backhand wrist muscles strong enough to hit a firm backhand.

Choosing a Grip—Because of all of the obvious advantages, I recommend that you try the one-grip system first. If it works, you will be rewarded by moments of brilliance and a great range of shots.

If it doesn't work, try a two-grip system with a modified Continental forehand grip and Continental backhand grip. If that fails, then try the standard two-grip system with an Eastern forehand grip and Continental backhand grip. Some players who use the two-grip system actually use the modified Continental grip as a third, intermediate grip during quick exchanges. In any case, never use the Western grip.

Because the grip size that is right for you is smaller in a racquetball racquet than in a tennis racket, there is actually much less difference between the Eastern and Continental grips than you will find in tennis. The smaller the grip, the smaller the difference.

Feel and Placement—Most players spread their fingers slightly to get extra

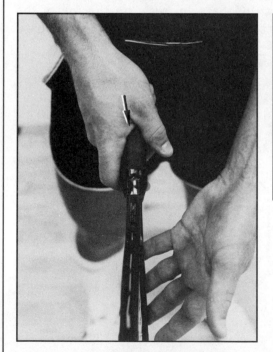

The modified Continental grip is shown here in two views. Notice that the crotch between thumb and forefinger is at the top part of the grip. Also notice that I prefer the "trigger" placement of my fingers.

"feel" no matter what grip system they use. The finger spread is often called the *trigger* grip because it resembles the grip used to hold a pistol. Other players bunch their fingers together in a *hammer* grip to allow for more wrist snap.

The racquet grip should be cradled in the palm of your hand. The butt should protrude slightly from the hand but should not stick out so much that you "choke up" on the handle. This will reduce power in your stroke.

Some players put the racquet butt in the palm of their hand. Power will increase from added leverage, but you will lose some control if you aren't a very careful player.

Your grip should be just firm enough to hold the racquet. It should not be hard and vise-like. A grip that is too tight creates tension, which slows your stroke and wastes energy. All you need is a slight squeeze during the downswing and impact phases of the swing.

FOREHAND DRIVE

The forehand drive is hit across the court or along the wall. You use it to move your opponent out of centercourt. The shot is most effective when it is hit sharply and strikes the front wall from six inches to two feet above the floor. It is sometimes called a *passing shot* because you can win a point by hitting the ball past your opponent.

The forehand drive consists of five phases—*preparation, windup, forward drive, impact,* and *follow-through.* Preparation allows you to start an early windup, so you have plenty of time to meet the oncoming ball. You should be in a semicrouched position, ready to spring into action.

The windup builds up the power of the stroke. Bring the racquet to head height or higher by first raising the right elbow to shoulder height and the forearm almost parallel to the floor. At the same time bring the wrist toward a fully cocked position. At this stage body weight is mostly on the rear foot—the right foot for right-handed players.

The forward drive unleashes the power generated in the windup, accelerating the racquet head toward the contact point. The right thigh thrusts the body forward while the right elbow begins its descent in a *pendulum* motion. This first brings the forearm into a vertical position and then levels out at the bottom of the pendulum trajectory with the upper arm pulling the forearm and racquet head behind it.

At impact, the momentum of the racquet head is transferred to the ball. The wrist snaps explosively just before impact to impart maximum power with equal deception. The ball leaves the racquet at a high velocity and in some cases with spin.

Finally, the follow-through ensures a complete transfer of momentum to

FOREHAND DRIVE IN TWO VIEWS
1) Regard the photo above and the one below as essentially two views of the same motion as you analyze them. Follow them from left to right. In the first set, the preparation phase is complete and the windup has begun. Notice how weight is mostly on the rear foot.

2) In the forward drive the racquet comes down toward the ball with the elbow dropping fast.

3) At impact, the power in the pendulum swing is transferred into the ball. Weight shifts to the front foot.

4) Follow-through allows you to watch the action, stay balanced and ready yourself for your opponent's return.

the ball and a balanced recovery from the shot.

The ideal forehand swing looks much more like a golf swing than a baseball swing. It *is not* a roundhouse motion in a plane parallel to the floor. Rather, it resembles a looping golf swing in a plane almost perpendicular to the floor. Let's look closer at each phase of the stroke.

Preparation—Without proper preparation, your swing will be rushed and often shortened, resulting in both lost power and control. Proper preparation begins with a semicrouched body, feet about shoulder-width apart, weight on the balls of your feet, and eyes on the ball.

Hold the racquet comfortably in front of you at about waist- or thigh-height. Use the backhand grip in the period between shots. This is important in the two-grip system when you may have to make a quick grip change.

The reason for always returning to the backhand grip between shots—even forehands—is that if there is insufficient time to change your grip, you can still use the backhand grip to hit a decent forehand. This isn't true of the forehand grip in a two-grip system used to hit a backhand shot. That's another good reason to adopt the one-grip system—the backhand grip is the same as the forehand grip.

Windup—A good windup gets the power flowing in the stroke. Although the windup is sometimes abbreviated during quick exchanges in forecourt, it is essential for maximum power and an effortless swing. You'll expend substantially more energy with an abbreviated-windup forehand than with a complete-windup forehand. Moreover, an abbreviated windup places a greater burden on the upper arm and upper body to generate speed in the racquet head.

The windup in the modern game can be executed very quickly. It consists of several stages that occur almost simultaneously. In fact it takes much longer to explain than to actually do it:

If you use the two-grip system, begin with a grip change from backhand to forehand. Change to the forehand grip by rolling the grip between your index finger and thumb. It is quick and easy because this is the natural inclination during the wrist-cock part of the stroke.

During the grip change, begin turning sideways so you face the right wall. Simultaneously, raise the racquet to about head height, or higher, by raising the elbow to shoulder height. At this point, the forearm should be nearly horizontal. The elbow should be bent at about 90°, putting the racquet head almost over your right ear.

Notice that you don't bring back the racquet first. Instead it is raised up and then back in a looping motion. This technique is quicker and generates much more racquet head speed than the classic method of bringing the racquet straight back.

Your wrist comes back fully cocked almost automatically. The looping windup motion naturally forces the wrist into position as the arm stops momentarily at the apex of the windup.

The windup should naturally place your weight mainly on your right (rear) foot. Your left shoulder should be slightly lower than your right shoulder as your upper body rotates down toward the contact point and slightly clockwise in a coiling action.

Time the windup so you are early enough to be ready for the ball, but not so early that you have to wait awkwardly for the ball to arrive. Experiment to find the timing that gives a moment of hesitation at the apex of your windup before accelerating the racquet and your body forward during the forward drive.

Forward Drive—The objective of the forward drive is to accelerate the racquet head to maximum velocity toward the contact point of the ball. Without the proper forward drive, the ball will float up and give your opponent an easy setup.

Begin by stepping toward the ball to make contact at a point slightly forward of your right shoulder. The contact point will vary, depending on the forehand grip that you use. For example, the contact point for an Eastern grip will be farther forward than for the modified Continental grip. In either case, though, it should not occur forward of your midsection. Otherwise you will lose power and end up with a less fluid swing.

For maximum control and power, step with your left foot so that your approach to the ball is both forward, toward the front wall, and slightly toward the right wall. The result is a slightly *closed stance*. During the forward drive, body weight transfers from the right (rear) foot to the left (front) foot as your hips and shoulders begin to uncoil.

During the forward drive, the arm swings down in a pendulum motion. The geometry of the swing looks like the letter *C* in an upright position. It's more of an up-and-down motion than a roundhouse motion. Knees and waist bend in adjustment to ball height.

During the downward flight of the racquet, the arm remains bent with the elbow tucked comfortably near the body. The arm does not straighten yet. The elbow is actually pulled down first, then forward.

Impact—Just before impact, the wrist snaps quickly from its cocked position. If the wrist begins to release too early or too late, the shot will be less powerful. The snap must occur quickly and be timed so the wrist is almost at the middle of the snap upon impact.

The arm remains slightly bent upon contact with the ball. This is important for absorbing the shock of the impact with the ball, preventing tennis elbow from developing. The racquet head should be perpendicular to the floor so you hit the ball almost flat. Such contact imparts all of the head speed to the ball. Some spin is possible, but it doesn't help you as it does in tennis.

Follow-through—A complete follow-through is essential for maximum transfer of momentum to the ball and also readies you for a defensive posture. The wrist completes its snap with the racquet coming straight through and over the left shoulder. The weight transfers completely to the left (front) foot. The hips uncoil completely so that they are now nearly facing the front wall.

The ball hits the front wall at a height of 24 inches or below, depending on whether it is a kill shot or passing shot.

SOURCES OF POWER

The forehand stroke described is efficient. You can hit balls at almost maximum velocity for hours with almost no arm fatigue. The key is the windup. A roundhouse motion doesn't capitalize on this endless source of power.

Consider why the pendulum of a grandfather clock swings back and forth seemingly forever on a single wind. It's the pendulum motion putting gravity to work. The same is true of the windup. Gravity helps accelerate the racquet head. A power player doesn't need massive muscles to make his shots fast and furious.

Steve Garvey on the Forehand

I've found that hitting a forehand—even chest-high shots—uses practically the same motions as throwing a baseball. A kill shot is like throwing a grounder, using a low, sidearm motion. A chest-high shot is like throwing a ball with a regular sidearm motion. A ceiling shot is like throwing a fly ball using an overhand motion. Improve the stroke for a forehand kill by using the looping windup Marty describes. But that part can be easily added to the normal throwing motion.

Wrist Snap—Another source of power is the explosive wrist snap. The windup brings the wrist to a full, laid-back position, ready to deliver power in an instant. You should hear a whooshing sound in your practice swings as the racquet head hits high gear.

The wrist snap is also necessary for control in quick exchange situations. Once the rest of the body is put into motion, it is almost impossible to change its initial course. The only way to make small adjustments in the ball speed or direction is by a quick change in wrist action. This makes sense because the wrist is held back until just before the ball contacts the racquet.

With a quickened wrist snap, you can send the ball crosscourt at the last moment if you see your opponent moving to cover the down-the-wall shot. Or, when the ball is coming so fast that you don't have time to take a full swing, use just the wrist to react quickly.

Hip Motion—Another source of power is the uncoiling of the hips accompanying weight transfer from the rear foot to front foot. Stand in place and sway back and forth to get the timing of the hip action. Notice the power inherent in hip motion. You'll see that arm strength has very little to do with generating power. In fact it is the last element considered in power hitting. Many beginners get sore arms and shoulders because they rely too heavily on arm swing and not enough on the other sources of power.

All of these elements must be timed so that they come into play at the best time. This takes practice and experimentation. You should adjust your timing during practice sessions, looking for the feel of the stroke. Great players spend months and sometimes years developing that perfect feel and execution.

NONIDEAL SITUATIONS

The modern forehand swing I've described outshines the more traditional swing in quick exchanges or nonideal hitting situations when you don't have time to set up properly. The player with the traditional swing is reduced to blocking or punching the ball in these critical circumstances. But the player with the modern forehand swing can still hit the forehand with authority. Chapter 18 covers championship shot-making and describes the technique of hitting offensive shots from an open stance and other nonideal positions.

THE KILL SHOT

The adjustments necessary to hit a kill shot instead of a passing shot are small in description but can seem huge in practice. In principle, the only difference between hitting a kill shot and a forehand drive is the height of the contact point and the levelness of the swing at impact.

You can hit a consistent kill shot only when contact is made with a level swing about six inches off the floor. Although you can hit kill shots from waist high, it's a low-percentage strategy. This is because the downward angle of the ball's trajectory usually causes the ball to pop up after hitting the front wall and then the floor.

The key to making a high percentage of kill shots is timing, once you have the mechanics of the forward drive mastered. Let the ball drop to about ankle height, ensuring that your swing is parallel to the ground when the racquet contacts the ball. Bend your knees and crouch down to the ball for maximum control. This is where the wrist plays a critical role. Because the ball is never hit exactly in the same spot relative to your body, the wrist must make the small adjustments necessary to insure that the ball's flight will stay low but not skip.

Try to hit forehand kill shots low. This keeps the ball traveling low, so there is little, if any, bounce after it hits the front wall.

Wrist snap must be just right or else the ball will rise or fall a few degrees, resulting in a passing shot or a skip ball. Thus, the kill shot demands the ultimate in precision and concentration.

I hope by now that you are convinced that the way to go is the modern swing I've described. You'll be miles ahead of the traditionalists if you use it.

DRILLS

Beginners enter the game of racquetball at various stages of athletic ability. They range from people who have never played sports to professional athletes from other sports. In either case, the effortless, modern forehand can only be attained by developing a feel for the perfect forehand stroke.

For some, this will entail many hours of simple drills to develop "memory" in muscles that have never before been taxed. For others, this will mean adjusting existing skills to the requirements of racquetball. No matter who you are, this section contains several drills to help you perfect forehand shots.

Grip Drills—The following drills will help you develop the proper grip and improve feel and control. As simple as these drills may seem, they are useful for inexperienced players and those who have never played a racquet sport.

Assume the proper forehand grip. Then try to bounce the ball up and down on the racquet face continuously. Use the forehand side of the racquet and make the bounces about 6 to 12 inches high. For best control, tap the ball. Use very little wrist snap, but just enough to keep the ball bouncing. These drills are intended to develop the feel of the ball, not the stroke.

Once you are able to keep the ball bouncing in the air about 50 times without it hitting the floor, try varying the height of the ball—a few low, a few high, and so forth.

Then repeat the drill using the backhand grip, bouncing the ball on the backhand side of the racquet.

After mastering these drills, move onto a court and stand about 10 feet from the front wall. Hit the ball to the front wall, soft enough and low enough so that the ball will bounce once in front of you after it rebounds. See how long you can continue this self-rally by counting the number of hits. Use a forehand grip, a forehand stance, and very little wrist action. Then repeat on the backhand side. As you become more proficient, move back 10 feet and repeat the drill.

You can also use the drill to practice grip change in the two-grip system. Tap a few backhands followed by a forehand. Then tap the ball back to the backhand side and repeat the process. This will get you used to using the backhand grip as the "home" grip you return to after every shot.

These drills are simple but necessary for those who have never played a sport requiring hand-eye coordination. The grip-change drill is useful if you are using the two-grip system for the first time.

Drop-and-Hit Drill—This is a good drill to develop the feel of the swing and to experiment with different aspects of the stroke. Stand in the center of the court about 30 feet from the front wall and face the right wall. Then drop the ball softly into the forehand contact zone and hit the ball about three to five feet high along the right wall.

Pick up the ball and repeat the drill. Try to find the timing and a contact point that make the shots feel good and natural.

After doing this drill for a few minutes, place a piece of tape about 3 or 4 feet high on the front wall. Try to hit the front wall below the tape, with the ball between you and the side wall. Repeat this 25, 50, or 100 times, depending on your inclination for practice.

Count the number of successful shots. Your success count will be an objective measure of your progress. When you are successful about 60 or 70 percent of the time, lower the tape on the front wall and repeat the drill. If you get really good at this drill, move closer to the right wall. This will give you a narrower lane along which to hit the ball. You can also use a crosscourt pattern in the drill.

Move-and-Hit Drill—This drill adds the element of movement to the drop-

and-hit drill. Find a willing partner if you want the most benefit from the drill.

Start deep in the centercourt area in the ready position. Your partner taps a soft setup to your forehand. You, in turn, step toward the ball and strike the ball either crosscourt or down-the-wall. As an alternative to tapping the ball with a racquet, have your partner throw the ball if he can't hit setups for you easily.

After you hit the ball, return to centercourt position while your partner retrieves the ball. Then repeat the drill. This exercise is not a rally, but a one-shot drill. By taking a short break between each shot, you will get a chance to think about how to improve on your previous shot.

Here, the backswing is chest high, which is too low. Power is sacrificed.

With a "roundhouse" swing your racquet arm swings too far horizontally. This is bad for balance and control.

When you have mastered this drill, try rallying with your partner. Practice shot patterns such as crosscourts back and forth to each other.

If you can't find a willing practice partner, you can still get many of the benefits of the above drill. Tap the ball softly to yourself to make the setup and make the shot as directed.

COMMON FAULTS

The accompanying photos and captions illustrate some common faults.

If impact with the ball is too far forward, you'll lose balance, power and control.

When the racquet face is not perpendicular to the floor, your shots will travel too high.

CHAPTER EIGHT

The Backhand

When I played my first national tournament in 1969, I noticed one thing about most of the players, even some of the top-ranked ones—their backhands were far inferior to their forehands. Often the backhand was used only in a do-or-die situation. Even today some pros have weak backhands.

I decided then and there that I would be a player with a balanced offense—a threat from either side. I practiced the backhand much more than the forehand. The results? A backhand that I think is more accurate and powerful than my forehand.

To have a balanced attack and prevent your opposition from picking apart your backhand, you too should spend a considerable amount of effort to make your backhand as big a threat as your forehand. Long-run benefits are numerous. Players always attack their opponent's supposedly weak backhand first. Very few players can recognize when an opponent has a better backhand than forehand. They revolve their entire game plan around one premise. If your game doesn't fit that mold, you will win more matches. It's that simple.

Luckily the backhand is not difficult to master. Conquering it requires mostly a psychological victory. We learn to bat forehanded, throw forehanded, and so forth. Popular mythology says that a backhand is difficult to learn—whether in tennis, ping-pong or racquetball. So when we get around to thinking about the backhand, we are already insecure about it.

In reality, the backhand *should be easier to hit than the forehand!* The mechanics of the backhand are in your favor because at the point of contact, your whole body weight is behind the ball, rather than in front of it as in the forehand.

Insecurity comes from the uncertainty of the untried and a lack of backhand muscle development. Hours of practice will kill the notion that a weak backhand is normal and, therefore, acceptable. It may be normal for you, but it is definitely not acceptable.

Backhand Grip—The backhand grip in the one-grip system is the same as the forehand grip—a modified Continental grip. The palm of the hand rests midway between the Eastern and Continental grip positions.

In the two-grip system, the backhand grip is either a full or modified Continental grip.

As in the forehand grip, most players spread their fingers slightly to get extra feel. But some players prefer to bunch their fingers together in a hammer grip to allow for more wrist snap.

All other aspects of the backhand grip are the same as the forehand grip. Recall that the grip should not be too tight, although you should squeeze the grip a bit more right before contact with the ball to ensure a firm hold on the racquet. At all other times, keep the grip fairly loose.

The contact point for the different backhand grips will be slightly different because of the natural orientation of the racquet head. Strive for a contact point that will give you a flat contact with the ball with the racquet face perpendicular

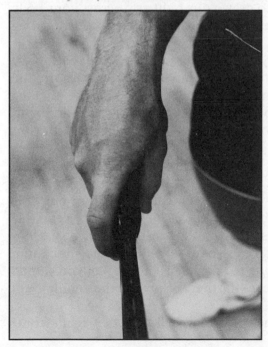

Most players use a Continental grip for their backhand. As discussed in the text, it's the preferred grip in a two-grip system. Also notice the "trigger" placement of the fingers.

to the floor. The contact point for the Continental grip should be a few inches closer to the front wall than with the modified Continental grip. In either case, the contact point should be about ankle to waist high and slightly forward of the leading (right) shoulder.

The backhand consists of the same phases as the forehand—preparation, windup, forward drive, impact, and follow-through. All of the basic principles used in hitting the forehand apply also to hitting the backhand except that the contact point is now forward of the body instead of deep in the stance.

But because of the different contact point, you have to make a few allowances in the stroke. The basic principles of the backhand are the same as those for the forehand. Major differences are shown in the photographs of the backhand stroke. However, let's review a few important highlights as they apply to the backhand.

Stroke Review—The main features of a good backhand include: a full windup, a pendulum swing, a powerful leg thrust into the contact zone, and an explosive wrist snap.

Preparation and Windup—As the ball approaches, begin the windup by drawing the right arm and racquet back along the perpendicular plane of the forward swing to come and bring the racquet behind your head. Meanwhile, your weight should be transferring back to your left (rear) foot.

Unlike the forehand, you will not be able to use the same looping motion to get into a full windup. You will have to draw your right arm across your body and up simultaneously. One common fault in this part of the stroke is to bring the racquet back too low.

Many racquetball teachers say that you should bring the racquet back early and hold the ready position. Unfortunately, if you follow this rule with the full pendulum swing, you will feel extremely cramped. You'll lose the rocking effect needed to get maximum windup. The only important preparation is to constantly shuffle the feet into proper position facing the left wall and with your weight ready to spring off the rear foot. The backswing should be timed so that you get maximum extension without holding yourself in an awkward set position.

At the apex of the backswing, the wrist is essentially straight up but fully cocked so the back of the hand is actually facing the back wall, ready to explode toward the ball. At this point, all the muscles from the waist up—which will contribute to the power component of the stroke—should be at maximum extension, like a taught rubber band ready to snap. This means that you should lift the racquet—now behind your left ear—farther up toward the ceiling right before you begin the downswing.

Rotate the shoulders away from the oncoming ball with the right (front) shoulder dropping below the left (rear) one as your upper body coils away from the ball. Shift the hips farther toward the left (rear) foot. Reach this position in one smooth motion and hold it for a split second.

Keep the wrist relaxed, almost floppy, when you take it back to its maximum extension at the apex of the backswing. This reduces wrist fatigue and lets you adjust easily to unpredictable shots. As the racquet begins its journey toward the contact point, pull the wrist back to its maximum extension in a fully cocked position.

If the ball is low to the ground, bend your knees and assume a semi-crouched position. If the ball is high, try to get high enough so that you can still use a pendulum swing. If the ball is so high that you cannot execute a pendulum motion, you should either hit a ceiling shot or hit down on the ball with little arcing motion.

Forward Drive—As you begin the downswing, squeeze the grip enough to get a firm grip, pull downward on the racquet, push off with your left (rear) foot, and accelerate toward the contact zone. Simultaneously, begin to uncoil your shoulders and hips. The contact zone should be in front of and slightly forward of your right knee.

Your motion toward the ball should put you into a closed stance. To keep the ball from sailing up, the right shoulder must level out just like the racquet trajectory.

A common fault is to shy away from the ball with the right shoulder above the left one and the follow-through high in the air. You can avoid this problem if you drive forward with your right shoulder leaning into the contact zone and with a complete follow-through. It carries your momentum toward the front wall.

Impact—In the final phase of the stroke, level out the swing just before impact, and snap the wrist with a level follow-through. The ball should explode from the racquet strings. If the stroke is not level with the racquet face perpendicular to the floor at the contact point, the ball will either skip or sail.

When you make contact with the ball, your arm should still be slightly bent to prevent tennis elbow from developing. However, the arm should be straighter than it is in the forehand stroke during the contact point. One common fault is that some players try to hit the backhand with a stiff arm. Another is that players point their elbow at the front wall and hit the ball far forward of the proper contact point. Both techniques will lead to an early case of tennis elbow.

Follow-through—The powerful thrust and step will tax the muscles in your right thigh. To relieve this strain, transfer the weight in the direction of the shot and follow through naturally. Snap the wrist so that the ball is hit almost flat. This will give you maximum power and minimize your chances for error when

BACKHAND DRIVE IN TWO VIEWS

1) Regard the photo above and the one below as essentially two views of the same motion. Follow them from left to right. In the first set, the preparation phase is complete and the windup has begun. Weight is mostly on the rear foot as the wrist and racquet are pointing practically straight up.

2) In the drive phase, weight shifts toward the ball with the elbow dropping fast.

3) Just before impact, level out the swing. At impact, snap the wrist as you keep the swing level.

4) In the follow-through, continue shifting your weight forward. Stay balanced and get ready for the return.

fatigue sets in. With underspin or topspin, the ball will float or skip when you get tired.

Timing, of course, is the key to hitting with maximum power while expending a minimum amount of energy. It can't be taught on a point-by-point basis. Rather, it must be learned by the "feel technique" in which you spend time on the court feeling the racquet make contact with the ball, experiencing the flow of the backhand swing. Always strive for a relaxed swing in which the arm moves freely without hitches or hesitation.

Summary—It should be obvious that the backhand stroke has many similarities to the forehand. This makes sense because they are based on the same basic principles. Both strokes use a compact but fully extended backswing and stress smooth weight transfer and body flow into the contact zone. Both demand an explosive wrist snap. In short, the strokes are extremely versatile because they avoid some of the archaic checkpoints demanded by classical strokes.

When practicing these strokes, stress timing and stroke creativity. In match play, the ball is hardly ever in a position where you can take the ideal stroke. Why force yourself into waiting for these few opportunities using an archaic swing? Create your own opportunities by learning to adjust to the situation at hand.

To beginners, this stroke may seem intimidating to learn, but that's only because the classicists say that it's impossible. Start hitting backhands with a free swing to develop backhand muscles. Then learn to adjust to changing situations by hitting backhands with lots of wrist snap. Finally, work on fully extending the backswing.

DRILLS

Modify the drills described for the forehand to develop your backhand. However, the toss in the drop-and-hit drill may be awkward at first because the ball toss gets in the way of the backswing. Try tossing the ball a little higher than you do for the forehand drop-and-hit drill. This gives you more time to wind up.

One note of caution, however. Make an extra effort to avoid contacting the ball behind your front (right) shoulder. Toss the ball so that you have to step into the ball to strike it.

This will help you avoid an insecure backhand because you will naturally hit the ball with authority, although not necessarily in the right direction. If you contact the ball behind your right shoulder, you will get into the habit of compensating for your skip balls by pulling away from the ball. This results in a loss of power and a floating ball.

COMMON FAULTS

The accompanying photos and captions illustrate some common faults.

Here, the backswing is too low and the arm too straight.

Knees aren't bent and too much weight is on the back foot.

If you hit the ball too far in front, you'll end up trying to "push" the ball. The shot will be weak.

I suggest that you never use a two-handed backhand stroke. You'll get much better results if you follow the method I use.

CHAPTER NINE

The Serve

Unquestionably, the most important shot in racquetball is the serve. Even so, few players realize the importance or the limitations of the serve. Basically the serve sets the tone of the rally. Don't expect the serve to always produce an abundance of aces.

With a good serve, a player can determine the course of the rally. He can make it a long, slow ceiling-ball rally or a short burst of quick shots.

This chapter covers four basic serves and a simple but effective service strategy. Mastery of these serves and the accompanying strategy will greatly improve your chances for controlling the course and the tempo of your matches.

FOUR BASIC SERVES

In my opinion, there are only four basic serves. Others are merely variations of them. When you combine the basic four serves with the three variables of ball speed, direction, and height, you'll have a big arsenal.

Here are the basic four:
1) Drive
2) High-lob
3) Half-lob
4) Z, or two-wall

Court Position—For starters, all serves should be hit from near the center of the service zone. This way it is easier to control centercourt.

You can relax this rule once your serves become truly devastating. For example, the Z serve to the right-rear corner is easy to execute if you move off center, closer to the forehand wall. If you have trouble controlling your serves, take a step away from the side of the court that you intend to serve toward, giving yourself a greater angle.

Basic Rules—To serve the ball, you must strike the ball after it bounces on the floor within the service zone exactly once. You may serve from any place in the service zone, but you must start and remain with both feet within the service zone until the serve crosses the short line.

The served ball must then hit the front wall and strike the floor behind the short line. The ball may hit one of the side walls after hitting the front wall, but if it hits two side walls after hitting the front wall, it is considered a fault.

Drive Serve—When struck very low and hard, the drive serve is akin to the cannonball serve in tennis. Both produce more *aces*—one-shot winners—than any other serve. You hit a drive serve with the same motion as a low forehand drive to one of the rear corners.

You don't have to be 6 feet tall and 200 pounds to hit an effective drive serve. In fact, you don't even have to hit it very hard. It is true that a power player can win points sometimes by just blasting one screaming drive serve after another. But the true master of the drive serve realizes that there are other factors, such as deception, that play a large part in an effective drive serve.

You should not try to hit the serve so hard that you are completely off balance. Your fastest drive serves should be hit with no more than about 90% of your maximum effort. If you are not strong enough to hit a drive serve that zooms past your opponents, don't worry. The most important quality of a good drive serve is that it is low. Ideally, if hit very low with sufficient pace, the ball will bounce twice on the floor before getting to the back wall and die near the rear corner.

This is an excellent serve to use against players who move slowly, are overweight, or are tall. The disadvantage of the serve is that if mishit, the ball can easily become a back-wall setup. Also, the serve affords you very little time to get into position for the next shot. Usually a series of quick exchanges follow this serve, and the rally ends quickly.

To get the most out of your drive serve, you should have a pair—a fast and an off-speed drive serve. This strategy is much like a baseball pitcher who uses a changeup after throwing a few smoking fastballs. The important point here is that it is the lowness of the ball that makes it difficult to return, not just the speed. Ball velocity helps, but it isn't the complete answer.

If the serve is low and slow, the receiver will not hit an effective return because his timing and reaction will be conditioned to the speed of the fast drive serve. There have been many times when I have seen a receiver caught flatfooted because he couldn't believe that the ball would move so slowly.

DRIVE SERVE
Form for the drive serve is similar to the forehand drive shot.
Generally, you hit the ball low, as shown from top to bottom.

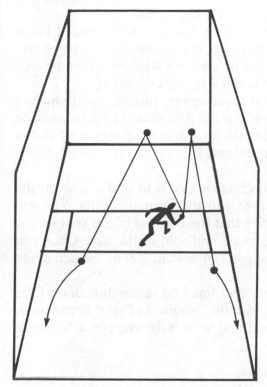

The drive serve hits the front wall low and travels to either rear corner.

Furthermore, you should vary the serve from side to side. But put most of the fast, drive serves on your opponent's weak side. An effective combination is to hit a few hard drive serves to the backhand, followed by a medium-speed drive serve along the wall on the forehand side.

When you do this, however, you should hit both serves with basically the same windup motion. The goal is to disguise the serves for as long as you can.

If you are a beginner, you will have to position your body so that it looks like you are going to serve to the forehand every time, even though you will serve to the backhand most of the time. Here's why: It is easier to hit across your body to the backhand side than to position your body for a serve to the backhand and try to hit to the forehand. Positioning yourself slightly to the right of center may also help you disguise your intentions.

High-Lob Serve—The high-lob serve is theoretically an exact complement to the hard, drive serve. It's high rather than low; soft rather than hard. Ideally, the high-lob serve should be hit as high into the air as possible, strike the floor somewhere between the short line and the five-foot line, and bounce into the back corner.

In another variation, the ball skims the side wall at a height of about six or seven feet and ten feet from the back wall before bouncing on the floor. This variation is more difficult to execute than the straight high-lob serve.

The high-lob serve is good for slowing down the pace of a game. I know that many beginners and some intermediate players consider it a sissy serve. But on the contrary, the high-lob serve can be a potent weapon. Many professional players use variations of it as their "bread and-butter" serve.

The advantage of the high-lob is that it requires very little energy to hit and gives you plenty of time to position yourself for the next shot. The disadvantage is that it requires great finesse to keep the ball away from the back wall and in the narrow lane that angles into the rear corner. It is definitely a control shot requiring hours of practice.

The best way to practice and hit a high-lob serve is to find a spot on the front wall where the ball should hit to give you the desired results. You will have to experiment to find this spot. Notice that the position of the spot on the front wall varies tremendously with the speed and spin of the ball. Once you have found this spot, try to aim for it and get a consistent feel of the ball every time you hit the serve.

When hitting the lob, stand with your feet lined up in the direction of the intended serve and push the ball upward with the uncoiling of your upper body. At the same time, your arm remains bent and your wrist stays in a laid-back position.

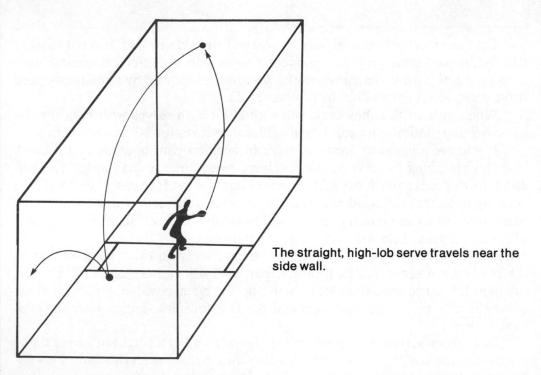

The straight, high-lob serve travels near the side wall.

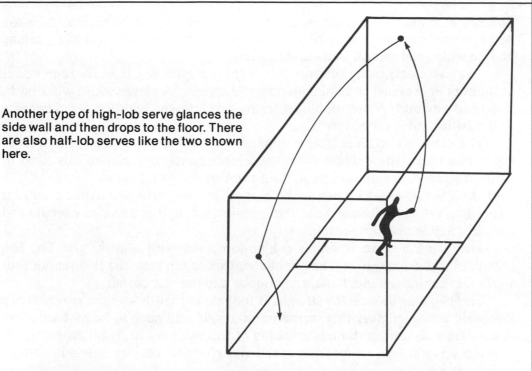

Another type of high-lob serve glances the side wall and then drops to the floor. There are also half-lob serves like the two shown here.

The racquet should contact the ball just slightly in front of the right shoulder. The lob can be hit flat, with underspin, or with topspin. But you will find that it is easiest to start with a flat, high-lob serve and slowly evolve into one with some underspin. The underspin allows you to hold the ball on the racquet longer and therefore gain a feel for the ball. The topspin, high-lob serve is the hardest to hit and should be avoided until much later, unless it is a natural shot for you.

Remember that the wrist should remain in its laid-back position during the entire service stroke. There is no wrist snap except for a very slight underspin motion. Even so, the wrist should not be so rigid that you are tense.

The arm should remain bent. This serve is hit with very little arm motion. The more arm motion you use, the less you will be able to control the serve.

The ball should be hit softly. For maximum effectiveness, ball contact should occur almost shoulder high so you can literally get underneath the ball and push the ball upwards with your legs and the soft uncoiling of your upper body. You will be able to control the ball much better if you bend your knees, and try to get underneath the ball. Weight should shift from your back foot to your front foot. Follow through by pointing the open racquet face in the direction of the spot on the front wall.

The serve is most effective against short players, players with a weak backhand, impatient players, and power players. A well-executed, high-lob serve to the backhand must be returned with a near-perfect backhand ceiling ball, in which ball contact is made at head height.

The extremely high trajectory forces short players to expend a tremendous amount of energy just stretching to return the serve. A player with a weak backhand will obviously have trouble returning a well-placed high-lob serve because of the critical timing required.

The serve is also ideal against impatient players and power players because the serve keeps the energetic, fast-rally opponent from playing his kind of game. You can win many points without even working up a sweat.

Half-Lob Serve—Also known as the *garbage* or *junk serve*, the half-lob serve is basically a valuable alternative to the high-lob serve. It is easier to execute and can yield almost the same result.

The half-lob serve is simply a high-lob serve with a lower arc. The ball should hit the front wall at a height of about six to ten feet, the floor about four to six feet behind the short line, and bounce into the rear corner.

The ball may be directed straight at the rear corner or into the rear part of a side wall. But remember that serves into the side wall need to be hit harder because side-wall contact diminishes some of the ball's speed. If hit properly, the half-lob serve should be medium speed and give the receiver only a head-high ball to return.

Unless hit perfectly, the half-lob serve is usually easy to return if the receiver is patient and hits a ceiling-ball return or if he is particularly adept at hitting shots at head height. However, most beginners and intermediate players can't stand the temptation a half-lob serve offers. They will try a kill shot, which is what you want them to do! In fact, most kill attempts from a half-lob usually end up as a setup for the server.

I use variations of the half-lob serve when I want a change of pace from the drive serve or as a second serve after a fault. I seldom expend the effort to try to hit a perfect high-lob serve. But this is not to say that the high-lob serve is a bad serve. I prefer to settle for a half-lob that varies between a high half-lob and a low one.

The advantage of this serve is that it is very easy to execute—so easy that you can probably serve a good one with a few minutes of practice. Its disadvantage is that a quick player can sometimes run up, short hop the ball, and drive the ball past you if you are not alert. However, he can't cross the five-foot line to do it, so you have a little protection.

Z Serve—This is a great shot to round out your bag of basic serves because it can win you many points. Because of the different bounces the ball takes, many players have terrible trouble returning Z serves.

It may be easier to hit the Z serve to the backhand from the left side of the

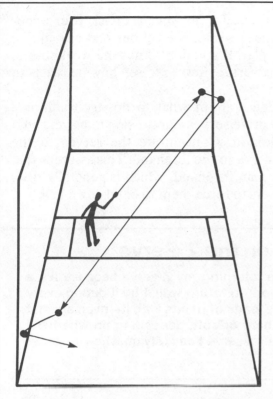

The Z serve takes so many bounces that it's tough to judge and return with authority.

court because you can get a better angle on the serve. In this case, the serve should hit about six to eight feet high on the front wall near the juncture of the right and front walls. Then it hits the right wall, bounces on the floor near the left rear corner, hits the left wall, and finally angles almost parallel to the back wall. For this reason it's also called the *two-wall serve*.

The serve must be hit sharply or your opponent may move up on the ball and catch you off guard and out of position. Furthermore, you need enough speed on the ball so that it will pick up spin as it bounces off the different walls. This also prevents it from angling off the back wall.

The disadvantage of the serve is that it comes through the center of the court, putting you momentarily out of position. Also, it is very easy to mishit the serve so that you hit the side wall first, resulting in an automatic sideout. Or the ball becomes an easy setup off the back wall.

SERVICE STRATEGY

General choices of service strategy are the same as the overall game strategy. You can either attack weakness, play to your strengths, or test your opponent's strengths.

The most successful service strategy for beginners is to stick to something simple that has worked well recently. Typically, this means attack your opponent's weaknesses. Ideally, you know these weaknesses either because you've played him before or have watched him play. If you don't know his weaknesses, you will have to discover them by trying various serves to see how he reacts to them.

Attacks—When you don't have any ideas about what to do, try traditional avenues of attack. For example, hit low drive serves side-to-side to players who are overweight, slow, or out of condition. Concentrate the serves to the backhand, but hit every third or fourth serve to the forehand. This assumes that your opponent has a weaker backhand than forehand, which is generally true. Use the drive serve against very tall players to force them to bend down low.

Steve Garvey on the Z Serve

A lot of my friends have trouble returning my Z serve because it's a confusing shot requiring good footwork to return well. I try it during every match. If I'm playing well, I can score loads of points with it—even against better players. I've learned to hit it hard or soft, depending on whether I want a fast or slow rally. So, for me, it's a serve I can rely on when my other serves are not scoring points.

Use one of the lob serves against players who have a weak backhand ceiling ball, a characteristic which seems to be true of most beginners. Also, use the lob serve against a power player to slow down the pace or against players who like to play a running, shooting game to keep them from playing their game. For every rule there is an exception. So if you can't find a traditional weakness, try something untraditional.

Once you have found your opponent's weaknesses, serve to them but try to vary the type and direction of the serves to keep him mentally off balance. Once you find a weak spot, his strengths usually deteriorate along with his confidence.

After serving, use the *one-second rule* in response to the service return. This rules says that you should go for a kill shot if:

1) Your feet are set for at least one second.

2) The ball is below your waist.

3) Your opponent is not already running up to the front wall to cover your kill shot.

As long as you move to centercourt to cover your shot, the results should be favorable.

EFFECTIVE SERVING

You can improve your chances for scoring if you follow these hints:

1) When you get into the service box, relax for a few seconds before serving. Take a few deep breaths even if you aren't tired.

2) Assess your opponent's physical and mental condition. Then choose the serve that promises the weakest return.

3) Before serving the ball, picture in your mind what the serve and the resulting rally will look like.

4) After hitting the serve, move as quickly as you can to centercourt.

5) Be ready for an offensive opening by watching, and anticipating your opponent.

6) If you get a chance, shoot the ball and recapture center court to await a possible return.

Developing Effective Serves—The key elements of an effective serve are to relax, assess, picture, move, watch, shoot, and cover. If you are a beginner, concentrate on these aspects. Starting with the first, try to add them one by one to your technique until they become part of your game.

Work on one serve at a time. I recommend that you start with the drive and half-lob serves and use them exclusively for about a month. In fact, try using one kind for an entire game just to practice that particular serve. As you become proficient at each serve, try a variation of it or a new one. For example, try off-speed drive serves, or soft Z serves. Try starting your service motion from different areas in the service zone.

The best way to develop an effective serve is to practice, practice, practice. As a beginner, you will have to build up a memory of front-wall spots, ball speed, and racquet feel for each serve you plan to use. This can only be done by first experimenting on the court with each serve to find the approximate front-wall target and service motion.

Drills—After you have narrowed down your idea about how a particular serve should be executed, you can begin serious practice. Mark key spots on the court where the serve should land. Then hit 50 or 100 serves, each time noting whether you have hit your targets. Make adjustments when you miss. Record the number of times you hit the targets to get an unbiased assessment of your serve.

As your serve improves, you may find that court targets need to be adjusted to account for improvements in your service skills. Certainly, as you play more, you will be able to hit drive serves harder, requiring you to lower the front-wall target area. This keeps the drive serve from rebounding off the back wall.

Or, you will learn to gently control the ball on the high-lob serve, requiring you to arc the ball higher and to move the front-wall target up higher.

In chapter 15, I describe service strategy for advanced players.

CHAPTER TEN

Other Bread-And-Butter Shots

Some players have a set of special, tricky shots. They look absolutely great during warmup—beautiful reverse-pinch overheads, unbelievable behind-the-back kills, and amazing side-to-side-to-front-wall kills. But when game time rolls around, these shots may not deliver.

Matches are won with a surprisingly small variety of shots. More points are won with the basic kill and drive shots than any others. These constitute the bulk of the "bread-and-butter" shots you must master to play winning racquetball. Only three others round out the bread-and-butter group: the near-side pinch, volley and ceiling.

The near-side pinch shot complements the down-the-wall shot. Hit the near-side pinch after you pin your opponent to the side or back wall. The volley is a surprise shot that often wins points through sheer positioning. And the ceiling shot, although defensive, is as indispensable as the serve.

You would be considered a fine, all-around player if you mastered just bread-and-butter shots. The exotic shots draw "oohs" and "aahs" from spectators, but the basics win points.

PINCH SHOT

The near-side pinch shot complements and enhances the down-the-wall shot because its coverage zone is diagonally across from the down-the-wall shot. Basically, the pinch is a kill shot hit into a front corner—side wall first. A *near-side pinch* is hit into the side wall in front of the player, while a *reverse pinch* is hit into the side wall behind the player. A forehand *near-side* pinch in this case would hit the right wall first, then the front wall. Pinch shots are illustrated on pages 41 and 47.

When hit with pinpoint accuracy, the pinch (near-side or reverse) is less returnable than a straight kill shot. Your opponent would have to be about six feet from the front wall to have a chance of getting his racquet on the ball. Typically, top players pin their opponents to the back wall with power drives and then make a quick, near-side pinch to end the rally. The opponent is trapped in backcourt. Beginners should avoid the reverse pinch until they have mastered the near-side pinch.

When you have great court position, even a high, soft, near-side pinch can be a winner. But most of the time, your opponent won't give you the luxury of waiting 10 or 20 shots for a chance to hit the pinch. The master of the pinch mixes it with passing shots to move his opponent the greatest distance. He then takes advantage of scoring opportunities by using a pinch or down-the-wall kill to end the rally.

Hitting the Pinch Shot—Hit the forehand, near-side pinch with the same motion as the forehand, down-the-wall kill. To get the most out of the shot, contact the ball deeper in your stance. For maximum control during normal-speed pinches, use very little spin, letting the walls add the necessary spin to keep the ball from popping up.

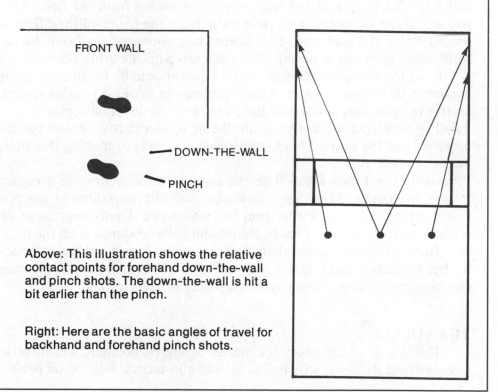

FRONT WALL

DOWN-THE-WALL

PINCH

Above: This illustration shows the relative contact points for forehand down-the-wall and pinch shots. The down-the-wall is hit a bit earlier than the pinch.

Right: Here are the basic angles of travel for backhand and forehand pinch shots.

When hitting a near-side pinch, wait a little longer than normal to catch the ball a few inches behind the normal contact point. This allows you to hit the ball into the right-front corner, using the same windup and delivery that you use for the forehand kill. This disguises your intention.

To hit a forehand, reverse pinch, use the same near-side pinch technique. Exception: You should assume an open stance so you can slide the ball into the left corner.

On slow pinch shots, slide the racquet face across the ball to impart some sidespin. Do this by dropping the face of the racquet below the wrist as you enter the normal leveling-off part of the stroke.

The spin allows you to feel or hold the ball and keeps it from popping into centercourt. Furthermore, hitting the ball with spin allows you to slow the ball down for a change of pace without changing your windup and delivery—the more spin, the slower the ball. But avoid a high follow-through. It could raise the ball into the air.

The higher the contact point, the less sidespin imparted. Almost all of the spin in a waist- or chest-high contact point is underspin. But the underspin should come from a natural wrist break, not an exaggerated one.

The pinch shot should contact the side wall from about one-half to three feet from the front wall and from one to six inches from the floor. The closer you are to the side wall, the farther away from the front wall and floor the ball should strike the side wall. This keeps your opponent far from the coverage zone, while minimizing the possibility of a setup off the other side wall.

In addition, a pinch hit from centercourt should be hit sharply, giving your opponent little time to react. This is imperative because your opponent is not far from centercourt and should have a view of the developing play.

The backhand pinch shot is hit like its forehand counterpart but from the other side of the court. There are no special secrets to making this shot, other than lots of practice.

Practicing the Pinch Shot—Use the same practice techniques recommended for the forehand and backhand, down-the-wall kill shots. Start by pinching balls that have been set up softly from the side walls. Then progress to pinching straight, oncoming balls. Finally, learn to hit balls rebounding off the back wall.

Stick with pinches, one right after the other. After you're comfortable with it, try mixing it with down-the-wall kills. When you have mastered this combination, you are a threat from anywhere on the court.

THE VOLLEY

The master of the volley is a master of angles, position, and surprise. He is a centercourt strategist with quick, hit-and-run tactics. Relying on perfectly disguised anticipation, he offers seemingly wide corridors of attack, only to run in with a counterkill here or power-drive parry there. He neutralizes the power player by punching quick volleys to the front corners and frustrates the control player by cutting off crosscourts with drive volleys to the opposite side of the court. He holds onto centercourt tenaciously.

The *volley* is any shot taken before it bounces on the floor. It is often called a *fly shot.* It's best to receive volleys in the region between the floor and your midsection. Higher shots should usually be allowed to travel to the back wall where they become simple setups.

There are many advantages in hitting the volley. First, and foremost, you can score quick points while expending very little energy. Second, you can maintain centercourt position and constantly pressure your opponent. Third, you can counter power and control with racquet skill and anticipation.

Because you are taking the ball at midcourt, you give your opponent much less time to recover. Usually your volley doesn't have to be very precise to be a winner. Even if he does recover in time to get to the ball, your opponent will have far less time to respond, testing his ability to accurately hit quick shots. This will put him on the run, forcing him to chase down every shot.

When to Volley—You have to decide quickly to volley. There isn't time to debate it with yourself. Knowing when to volley comes through experimenting

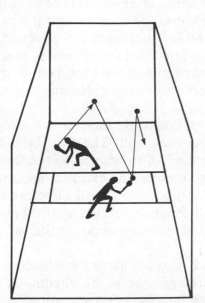

If you read a crosscourt shot and you are in centercourt, move up to volley the return into backcourt.

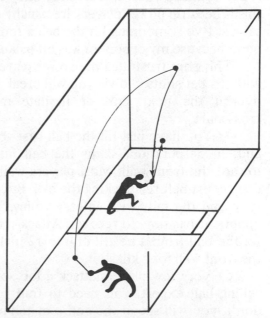

Weak returns off of the back wall should be put away with a volley.

and split-second decision-making on the court. A few rules of thumb extracted from playing situations can also help:

1) If your opponent is almost lying on the floor in the forecourt after barely returning your shot, try to end the point by driving the ball away from him with a volley. Try it even if it means leaping into the air to hit a ball that is over your head.

If your opponent is not out of position in the forecourt and your volley is inadequate, then take a high ball off the back wall unless you are just trying to practice the volley.

2) Your opponent is in front of the short line and drives a high, crosscourt shot while you are in centercourt. If he telegraphs his intentions even slightly, step to the right, cut off his return, and volley the ball down the right wall. The shot doesn't have to be impressive because your opponent is out of position. Your opponent has a chance of returning the shot only if you hit the ball too hard or too high and the ball comes off the back wall.

Keep the ball off the side wall because it could slow the ball enough to give your opponent time to recover.

3) Power players have a tendency to hit fast drive shots from backcourt. If your opponent fires a blistering crosscourt within your reach, step in and softly volley the ball into the corner. Even if he hits a crosscourt power kill that has already bounced once, this type of volley can still be used to kill the ball. Typically this is because power players are usually off balance after uncorking one of their salvos. I've sometimes hit the ball a foot high into the corner and still won the point because my opponent was off balance and far from the coverage zone.

This shot frustrates the power player and puts doubt in his ability to score with his pet shots. Slowly you will break his rhythm because he will either try to overhit the next shot or hesitate momentarily before blasting his next crosscourt.

4) You have just hit the ball past your opponent. He scurries to backcourt and, in desperation, slams the ball into the back wall. The ball floats high toward the front wall. Most players wait for the ball to bounce on the floor in deep court before attacking the ball. But they've missed an excellent opportunity to end the rally with an easy volley. You should volley the ball before your opponent has time to recover. Attack the ball. Position yourself so that you can hit the ball from a height of 6 to 12 inches and then firmly punch the ball into the front wall for a kill shot.

5) Very few players attack a lob serve. If you are playing a lob-serve and ceiling-ball expert, you need to find something to break his rhythm. If you don't, you will spend the entire match pinned into the left-rear corner, literally crawling the walls.

A volley is the perfect answer. Move up to the five-foot line and drive the

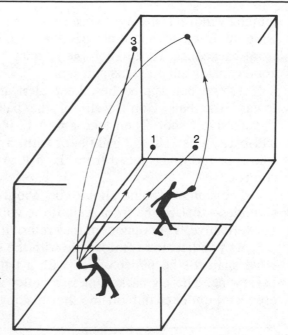

Consider returning weak lob serves with volleys (1) down the line, (2) crosscourt or (3) to the ceiling.

ball down the left wall. If you mistime your approach, punch the ball to the ceiling instead. Not only have you changed the rhythm of the game, you've put pressure on your opponent. The ball doesn't have to be hit very hard when you're at the five-foot line because you're close to the front wall. Your opponent will still have very little time to react.

In these situations, the volley should be used. But there are also other situations where it can improve your scoring opportunities.

How to Hit the Volley—A beginner should punch his volleys. Precision and control are most important, not power. In the situations cited earlier, notice that power and speed are never mentioned—only accuracy. In most cases, you can rely on the speed of the oncoming ball. Only in the advanced *drive volley* do you need to power the ball.

Begin by using a backhand grip for both the forehand and backhand volleys. There's usually no time to change grips when hitting the volley. That's why I stressed returning to your backhand grip as your home grip.

Learn to hit the forehand volley from both closed and open stances. During a quick exchange, you may not have time to move your feet. In either case, you should bring the racquet up about a foot higher than the ball with your arm bent at about a 45° angle. If the ball is low, you may have to bend your knees to get down to the ball. As you bring the racquet into position, cock the wrist.

The beginner's volley is a punching motion with very little backswing. The looping windup is not used because there's no time for the beginner to properly wind up. Even advanced players don't wind up except when the ball is traveling from backcourt. Try to keep the racquet head above the wrist. This gives you good control and prevents pop-ups.

As the ball approaches, keep alert and watch it. If you have time, step toward the ball. Don't wait for the ball to come to you—a volley is an "aggressive" shot. Then take a 6-to-12-inch *punch* at the ball with a stiff, but laid-back, wrist. Hit the ball flat or with slight underspin. In this case, excessive spin robs too much speed from the ball. Avoid that except when you need the control.

The contact point should be about 12 inches in front of your right shoulder—toward the front wall. If the volley is hit too defensively, it won't be very effective. Your opponent may return it, putting you on the defensive.

As you become comfortable with the stiff-wristed punch volley, add some wrist snap to the punch. Stick with a flat contact, but stay away from a big backswing. The big backswing in a volley is reserved for the drive volley, covered later under championship shot-making.

Steve Garvey on the Volley

Hitting a beginner's volley is like bunting. Keep your eyes on the ball. Move up or down with it. Learn to make solid contact first before adding refinements. Use a short punch to direct the ball where you want it to go. The volley, like the bunt, doesn't have the "pizazz" of a power drive, but it can score points just as easily.

Practicing the Volley—The volley is difficult to practice without a good partner because the ball must be set up carefully. The best way to practice the volley is to have a teaching pro or advanced player hit soft setups to you.

If you want to practice alone, try this drill: Stand in centercourt either at the short line or in the service zone. Then hit a half-lob serve toward your forehand volley zone. Step toward the ball and punch it down the right wall. After practicing the forehand volley, half-lob to the backhand side and volley the ball down the left wall.

The biggest mistake that beginners make is to abandon the punch volley because it doesn't have the same zip other shots have. Some advanced players flail at their volleys, hitting with everything they have. But if you get a chance to watch a professional match, notice that they use a "wristy" punch with a short backswing. Remember that it is a quick shot made when your opponent is out of position.

CEILING SHOT

In bygone days of racquetball, the ceiling shot was an offensive weapon. Players would make the shots so precise that they would hug the side walls and pin their opponents in the back corners. But this was when balls were less lively and players less skilled. Ceiling-ball masters won by dictating every move in their matches. Rallies of 20 or 30 shots were common. Patience and orderly rallies prevailed.

The ceiling shot has lost its exalted rank in the modern game, but it is still essential. In fact, at lower skill levels, the ceiling shot is still a potent offensive weapon. In the modern game, the ceiling shot is used to neutralize a variety of offensive shots. That's because there is no adequate response to a good ceiling shot except another well-placed ceiling shot. Therefore the power player and the control player respond similarly once a ceiling rally starts.

Hit the ceiling shot into the ceiling about one to five feet from the front wall. Ceiling balls should normally be directed to your opponent's backhand. Ideally, the ball should travel in a high arc close to, but not touching, the left wall until it drops into the left-rear corner. There, your opponent must hit a backhand ceiling shot from shoulder height.

How to Hit the Ceiling Shot—Stroke the forehand ceiling shot with an overhand motion resembling a baseball player throwing a ball toward the ceiling. Use a standard forehand grip and either a straight-on or open stance. All the

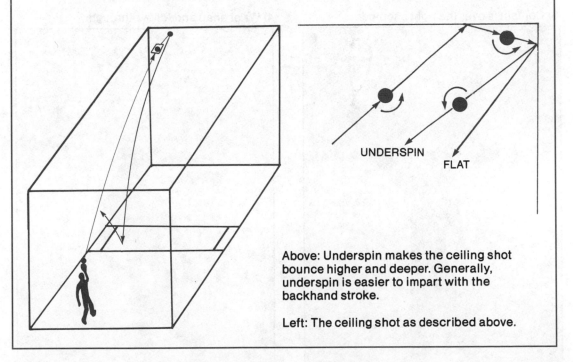

UNDERSPIN
FLAT

Above: Underspin makes the ceiling shot bounce higher and deeper. Generally, underspin is easier to impart with the backhand stroke.

Left: The ceiling shot as described above.

FOREHAND CEILING SHOT
1) Overhand motion begins.

2) Weight transfers forward.

3) Contact is over the right shoulder.

4) Wrist snap and follow-through.

BACKHAND CEILING SHOT
1) The basic stroke is underhand.

2) The shoulder and elbow lead the stroke as weight shifts forward.

4) Try to impart underspin with the wrist snap and follow-through.

3) Contact the ball at about shoulder height.

basic principles of shot-making—wrist cock, weight transfer, wrist snap and good follow-through—apply in this shot too.

A few adjustments will improve the shot: Try to get underneath the ball and arch your back so you can let your stomach and leg muscles aid in propelling the ball to the ceiling. If necessary, move toward the front wall to get into the right position. By contacting the ball over and almost behind your right shoulder, you can hit the ball with less effort because of the angle. Because the ceiling shot is a medium-speed shot anyway, this is OK. Little power is necessary to hit a properly timed ceiling shot.

Hitting underneath the ball imparts some natural underspin. This can improve the quality of your ceiling shot. If you can impart some underspin, the ball has a higher trajectory after bouncing on the floor and will be tough to return.

You can also hit the ceiling shot from a lower posture and with different motions. What I have described is a technique for hitting an effortless forehand ceiling shot. You can hit this ceiling shot over and over and not tire because you use stomach and leg muscles to assist arm and upper-body muscles.

Hit the shoulder-high, backhand ceiling shot just like a normal backhand, except that the contact point is about shoulder high. Try to put some underspin on the ball. This way you don't have to hit the ball as hard. Practice strengthens your backhand muscles, sharpens timing and makes the backhand ceiling shot effortless. Although the head-high ceiling shot takes less effort to hit, it is an advanced shot requiring critical timing to execute.

I can't overemphasize the importance of a fluid swing, proper contact point, and complete follow-through in hitting the backhand. Beginners tend to be meek and too defensive about it.

Practicing the Ceiling Shot—If you are a beginner, practice the ceiling shot by hitting it down the middle of the court until you can carry on a 10- or 20-shot ceiling rally with yourself. Then move the target area a few feet closer to the left wall. Repeat the drill, working your way to a narrow five-foot corridor along the left wall.

SUMMARY

There you have it—all the bread-and-butter shots necessary to play a winning game of racquetball. By now you may be wondering about the overhead and the around-the-wall ball. Forget them. Quality of shots, not quantity, is what counts. I discuss how to defend against those and other shots later but, in short, they're mostly good for show and emergencies, but almost useless as basic point-makers.

CHAPTER ELEVEN

The Service Return

If the serve is the most important shot in racquetball, then the service return must be the second-most important shot. You need a good serve for conquest—and an equally good return for survival. This is because you cannot score a point while returning a serve, putting you at the mercy of the server.

When you return a serve, your first task is to neutralize your opponent's offensive advantage. You want to at least be even after the return. Your second task is to win back the serve and then score points.

It is no wonder that a good service-return game is based on a good backhand ceiling shot. The best servers always test their opponent's backhand first—lob serves to test the high backhand and drive serves to test the low backhand. Until you can return almost any serve to the ceiling, you will spend most of your time in backcourt either pinned against the rear corner or on the floor trying to dig out drive serves.

KNOW YOUR LIMITS

You must know your offensive limits or suffer the consequences. Either you won't win enough service returns or you will lose too many rallies on poor returns. For example, I know that my best shot is to kill down the line any drive serve to my backhand. But it probably is not the best choice for you unless you have a very good backhand. If you have not mastered the ceiling return yet, you will lose more points than you will win if you use non-ceiling returns. Perhaps a few drives or kill shots to keep your opponent honest will be necessary, but beginners should *use* the ceiling shot until it's mastered.

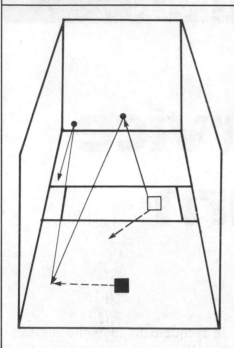

If you can, return the serve with a kill shot. In this case a down-the-line shot finds the server way out of position.

This advice may seem confusing. Here's my reasoning: When you are receiving serve, you are totally on the defensive. To hit a winner, you have to practically make unplayable rollouts. By returning the serve with a ceiling ball, you get yourself out of a defensive position and neutralize your opponent's chances to take the offensive. Also, your opponent must leave centercourt. The ceiling ball return does not have to hug the side wall to be effective—it has only to get to backcourt.

A beginner should be mentally conditioned to return all serves to the ceiling. It should be automatic. When you are tired, you can't afford to spend time deciding what type of return to hit. If you normally go for a kill shot, you will try a kill when you are tired. But when you are tired, kill shots will be worse than usual. The result is lost points, just because of poor service returns.

STRATEGY

For practice, try returning every serve with a ceiling ball. As mastery develops, so does confidence. Your opponent will be pressured into trying to hit winners.

After mastering the ceiling return, start thinking offensively. Change your strategy to keep your opponent guessing. Attack the serve and either forcefully drive the server out of centercourt or put the ball away outright.

Half-Volley Return—On slower serves, such as shallow lobs and "junks," move up and half-volley the serve for a kill, pass or ceiling shot. A *half-volley* is a ball hit immediately after it bounces on the floor.

Coming up on the ball can surprise your opponent and be very intimidating if he hasn't seen the shot. I've seen many a junk-serve expert give up the serve after seeing it killed repeatedly.

Even if you decide that you can't kill the ball as you approach it, there's plenty of time to hit the ball into the ceiling. The half-volley ceiling ball is also effective. It travels much faster to backcourt than a normal ceiling ball. A slow server will have to rush his shot.

Returning Sucker Serves—The kill/pass/ceiling rule applies as well on the service return: Kill if you can, pass if you must, hit a ceiling if you have to. The difficulty is the *if you can* part of the rule. You are in the worst defensive position when returning serve—and the server knows it. That's why he will often give you a *sucker serve*—one that seems to be a tantalizing setup but in fact is not.

What would normally be a setup during the course of a normal rally is not necessarily one during the service return. The returner is 35 feet from the front wall. The server is less than 20 feet away. The returner is on the run; the server is not.

A shoulder-high half-lob or Z serve is often used to lure the kill instincts out of an impatient player. After hitting one of these sucker serves, the server looks for a kill return that he can cut off and punch low into a corner. Notice

If you can't kill, try a passing shot. Here, a crosscourt works well.

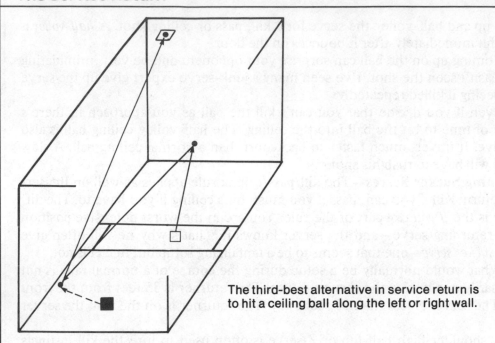

The third-best alternative in service return is to hit a ceiling ball along the left or right wall.

that it takes him a step and a lunge to do this. It would take you at least seven steps to return his shot if your return is high.

The only way you can find out if you should try the kill is to do it a few times. Even if it is less than perfect, you have accomplished two things: 1) You have given notice that you will not let him relax. 2) You find out if he is capable of covering a drive return.

Summary—Some players do not take their serving advantage seriously enough and tend to stand in the service zone after hitting the serve. The best return against this type of player is to shoot or drive the ball, leaving him standing in the service zone.

Develop a good ceiling return. Then begin attacking the serve until you feel that you are losing too many points on poor returns. Finally, back off slightly to find the proper offensive and defensive mix.

READING THE SERVE

The motion of your opponent's wrist is the key to reading the serve. The wrist snap cannot lie. Where the wrist goes, so goes the serve.

Forget all of the feet shuffling, hip wiggling, and arm pumping your opponent shows during the serve. If the wrist snaps early, the serve is going crosscourt. If it snaps late, the serve is going down the line. If the wrist snaps very early, it's going to be a Z serve. And if it snaps very late, the serve is going to be a Z in the other direction.

Watching the wrist snap is also a good way to concentrate during a match. If you can't remember which way the wrist snapped on the last serve, you're probably daydreaming.

Technique—Stand about two or three steps in front of the back wall and midway between the side walls. You may want to experiment before deciding on a primary spot to stand.

For example, very quick players sometimes like to stand closer to the service zone so they can jump on the ball and catch the server off balance with a drive. Shooters like to stand closer to the back wall so they can get a little more time to set up. You may also have to move a step left or right to get a good view of the serve.

Assume a comfortable, crouched position with your knees slightly bent. Hold the racquet in front of your knees and use a backhand grip. Try to determine if the serve is be soft or hard. If soft, assume a less-crouched position. If hard, crouch lower as the server goes into his motion. Watch his wrist!

As the ball is struck, decide what kind of serve it is and respond accordingly. If it is a drive serve, save valuable time by using a *crossover* motion. The foot farther from the coverage zone steps across the body. For example, to cover a drive serve to the left, your right leg should step across toward the left wall. This motion saves an extra half step and puts you naturally into a closed stance.

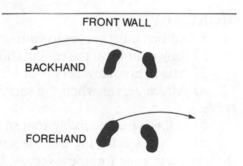

FRONT WALL

BACKHAND

FOREHAND

Above: To cover the greatest distance in the shortest time, step *across* your body.

Left: When receiving the serve, it's best to stand a few steps in front of the back wall, equidistant from the side walls.

Bring the racquet up to shoulder height and the wrist to a relaxed, cocked position. As the ball approaches, go through the normal windup. Watch the ball carefully, especially for irregular bounces.

On the backhand side, you will find that you can turn almost facing the back wall and still hit an effective return. However, if you are in an open stance, it is almost impossible to hit the backhand with any power during a service return.

If your opponent is hitting low drive serves that are hard to return even with a ceiling shot, try slicing the ball to the ceiling with lots of underspin. A flick of the wrist is all that's needed to return a hard drive serve. You can use the speed of the serve by translating the horizontal speed to high-velocity spin, causing the ball to shoot off the ceiling and rebound in a high arc to backcourt.

Steve Garvey on the Service Return

I don't try to do too much with the service return, and I don't expect much from it—except avoiding a setup for my opponent. I think this attitude has reduced my service-return errors. But that doesn't mean I hit the ceiling all of the time. I just don't get upset when I don't end the point on the return. Many players expect too much from the return. Most players will give you ample other opportunities to end the rally to your advantage.

MORE ADVICE

1) Return most serves to your opponent's backhand.

2) Rely mainly on the ceiling shot to counter drive serves.

3) Attack low, slow serves or serves that set up in the middle of the court.

4) Attack serves when the server tends to stay in the service zone after the serve.

5) Adjust your receiving spot so you can get a good view of the serve.

6) If you are having trouble with returning a drive serve, move closer to the coverage zone for a few serves. Do this even if it means leaving one side of the court open. This tactic forces the server to try a different serve for a while and may break his rhythm. Return to your normal receiving spot after you force the server to try a different serve.

7) If you are getting jammed by a Z serve, stay in the center of the court longer. Keep alert and shuffle your feet in preparation for a weird bounce.

8) If you are having trouble with high lob serves to the backhand, try one of three things. One, move up and take the ball out of the air. Hit a ceiling shot or drive it. Two, turn your back more to the front wall and swing with a higher

arcing motion. Three, try to slice the return to the ceiling instead of hitting it flat.

9) This may sound strange, but if you stand slightly pigeon-toed while receiving serve, you can get a better jump on drive serves.

10) Select a return that drives your opponent out of centercourt or wins the rally outright.

PRACTICING SERVICE RETURNS

Find a partner who wants to practice both the serve and the service return. Select two or three serves to practice. While one player practices serves, the other player can practice returns. Practice the backhand ceiling return first. It's the safest shot. Then start attacking the serve with natural, fluid strokes.

Stick with one serve for about 10 minutes. Doing this gives enough repetitions so you can begin to "feel" the return, yet not so long that you get bored and practice the same bad habits over and over. Then try a different one.

Try to help each other out. It doesn't do the returner much good if the server can't hit a decent serve. And it gives a false sense of accomplishment to the server if the returner can't return a simple serve. Take time between serves to mentally review the previous shot and what adjustments might be appropriate.

The quick windup and release of the modern forehand and backhand should give you an advantage against a "classic" player. Add to that a quick wrist and you have the physical tools necessary to use an offense-oriented, service-return strategy.

CHAPTER TWELVE

Footwork, Bodywork And Playing The Walls

For beginners, the most perplexing situations arise when the ball bounces off the back or a side wall. Advanced players enjoy the challenge. Beginners typically don't know what to do and stay frozen to the floor. Advanced players see a scoring opportunity. Beginners see only the difficulty of the unfamiliar bounce, the embarrassment of tangled feet and the smirks of a knowing opponent.

Like the backhand, these difficulties can be overcome. You need to become familiar with angles and bounces and develop the basic skills required to respond to each situation.

This chapter teaches you how to move to the ball. More accurately, it shows you how to move away from the ball. You will learn how to run and how to shuffle. This is the essence of proper *footwork*. Using your body to gain good court position leads to offensive *bodywork*. Both can help get you out of tough shot-making situations. They also help you widen scoring lanes, giving you greater margins for error.

FOOTWORK

Good footwork is a prerequisite for speed in responding to awkward bounces, balance while approaching the ball, and power during the stroke. Good footwork and the modern pendulum swing make a dynamite combination. They help you deliver the best shots under the most trying conditions.

Position—Good footwork begins with a good defensive position—feet about shoulder width apart, weight on the balls of your feet, knees bent enough for good balance, and head up. Be light on your feet with a slight bounce on your toes, ready to push off in a flash in any direction.

You should spend some time working on developing a comfortable, but efficient, defensive position. Stand in your living room, or on a court, and practice bouncing in place. At first, this can be quite taxing on your legs, but you will quickly get used to it as you strengthen them.

This bouncing motion is not jumping. You should not leave the floor. It is a continuous flexing of the knees designed to keep the weight on your toes and the leg muscles ready to spring into action. Practice springing into a closed stance by stepping across your body to the right or to the left.

Good footwork continues with a *shuffle* run or a sideways *jog*. They are used in moving toward or away from the ball on setups. Such maneuvers allow you to move quickly toward or away from the ball yet still let you take a good swing at the ball while on the move.

For example, as you approach the ball, you will need to make minor body adjustments, but you don't want to turn away from the ball or get your feet tangled. The shuffle run and the sideways jog allow you to do this.

Shuffle—The shuffle looks like a sideways hop. You thrust to one side with one foot, hop, and bring the trailing foot next to the lead foot.

For example, if the ball is coming off the right side wall, and you need to move back a few steps, turn to face the right wall. Push back with your left foot and step sideways—toward the back wall—with the right foot. Then bring the left foot almost next to the right foot.

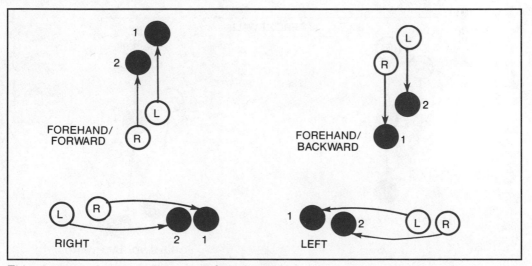

This shows the basic shuffle step in four directions.

If you need to move back farther, just repeat the maneuver by pushing back with the left foot again. During the entire movement, your body should be semicrouched in a closed stance, ready to strike the ball. The maneuver resembles a gliding motion.

Sideways Jog—When you have to travel a long distance to the ball, you should run normally at first. Then go into a shuffle when you get within about 10 feet of the ball. The shuffle and sideways jog are meant for making minor positional adjustments, not covering long distances.

The sideways jog is an advanced method for running while facing a side wall or maintaining a closed stance. The footwork depends on which wall you intend to face and whether you want to move up toward the front wall, or back toward the back wall.

On the forehand side, if you want to move up, push off with your right foot, swing your right foot behind the left foot, and finally step with your left foot toward the front wall. After the second step, your feet are actually positioned so that you would naturally have your back to the front wall. But this is just an extreme form of a closed stance. If you want to move back, push back with your left foot, swing your left foot in front of your right leg, and step back with your right foot. The footwork on the backhand side is the same as on the forehand side.

Footwork Drill—The following drill will limber up your footwork. Get on a court or any rectangular area. Stand in the right-rear corner and face the right wall. Shuffle or jog sideways toward the front wall, while facing the right wall.

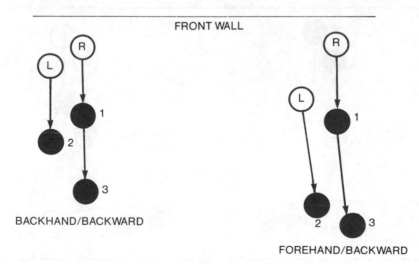

The sideways jog looks like this.

Touch the front wall and shuffle or jog sideways back to the back wall, still facing the right wall. Then repeat the exercise along the left wall. Or try shuffling around the court.

After a few sessions, the racquetball shuffle and the sideways jog will be second nature to you and you won't have to worry about getting your feet all tangled up when preparing for your shots. You will be much more mobile and more prepared to address the most difficult shots.

Steve Garvey on Footwork

The shuffle is found in any sport requiring quick adjustments while facing a particular direction. Baseball infielders use it all the time to field grounders. Basketball players use it on defense while guarding an opponent. Obviously, tennis players use it at the baseline. It takes only a few minutes to get used to if you practice it alone. Jumping rope helps strengthen leg muscles to make shuffling easy.

PLAYING THE SIDE WALLS

You should be able to approach side-wall shots with much more confidence with your new mobility. One more drill will prepare you for handling any side-wall shot you are likely to encounter.

The biggest mistake made by beginners is that they rush toward the ball when they should be moving away from it. On side-wall shots, you should position yourself so the ball can be struck from below the chest.

Sometimes this is not possible. But you should still strive for this position if you can. If you can't, then hit a ceiling shot or volley the ball along a side wall. Quick positioning starts with good anticipation. Try to read your opponent's shot early. Then move far enough back and to the side so that you can still step into the shot. The step toward the front wall is crucial for adequate power.

Drill—Stand in your centercourt spot without a racquet. Face the front wall while your partner stands next to the receiving line on the left wall. Have him hit or throw a soft, 10-foot-high shot that hits the front wall and then rebounds off the right wall toward centercourt.

Watch your partner. As soon as the ball leaves your partner's racquet, turn to face the right wall and shuffle into a position where you can take one or two steps toward the ball and catch it below your waist. When you can do this successfully most of the time, pick up a racquet and repeat the drill. This time hit the ball down along the right wall.

The drill, without racquet, will teach you that you can move into backcourt and still have time to reach the ball. You will also learn to read angles.

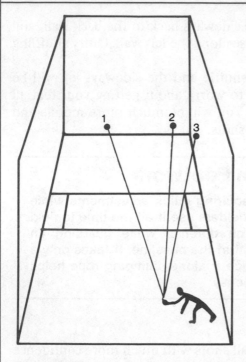

A high ball that travels through centercourt may trap you deep near a side wall. If so, you have three good options—(1) a crosscourt kill, (2) a down-the-line kill or (3) a reverse pinch to the near side.

Moreover, you will be much better positioned to hit the ball with authority because you will be stepping into each shot and striking it in your power zone, the region between your waist and knees.

After you have gained enough confidence without worrying about swinging a racquet, the drill with the racquet in hand will be much simpler. Your movements should be almost natural. Mental energy will be channeled into combining your stroke and your footwork.

PLAYING THE BACK WALL

The skills acquired while learning how to respond to side-wall shots also apply to back-wall shots. However, the court movement will be first toward the back wall, and then toward the front wall.

For the moment, consider the forehand: After you see that the ball will rebound off the back wall, follow it back toward the back wall. Move just enough so you are positioned two or three steps behind the point where you will contact the ball. Then prepare for the shot in the usual manner as it approaches you from the back wall. Bend the knees and begin a forward shuffle or sideways jog, following the ball toward the contact zone. Just before you reach the contact zone, execute the forehand in the normal manner.

Beginners usually make one of two big mistakes when playing back-wall shots. They either stand and watch the ball without preparing for their shot, or they run so far back toward the back wall that they have to chase the ball after it hits the back wall.

These positioning errors can be corrected if you understand the best court positions for back-wall shots. Modify the side-wall drills so you can practice spotting the best contact zones. Once you understand the bounce of the ball, you will be able to hit the ball with much more zip and with greater accuracy.

SHOT SELECTION AND BODYWORK

In most cases, the basic rules of shot selection still apply for side- and back-wall shots: Make your opponent run the longest distance. And make your opponent run through your position. But there are also situations offering alternatives.

Suppose that a ball is bouncing into centercourt from the left. Should you use a forehand or a backhand? In most cases, use a backhand. You can keep your eye on the ball during its entire flight, and it is always easier to hit a ball coming into your body than one coming across your body. If the ball is coming from the right wall, use a forehand.

The following situations illustrate how to apply the above rules of thumb:
Situation 1—Your opponent hits a high shot from the right that comes off the left wall. Move toward the right-rear corner of the court and then step into your shot. If your opponent stays on the right side of the court, hit the ball down the left wall because he will be pinned against the right wall. However, if he quickly darts over to the left side of the court, hit it down the right wall.

In most cases, he will not have time to dart across the court. Advanced players will sometimes fake a quick backhand volley to freeze opponents on the right side of the court. Then they psychologically push them toward the right wall by quickly backpedaling into proper court position. This is a legitimate and effective maneuver designed to break your opponent's rhythm and force him to take a few extra steps. Although you will take more steps than he will, his unplanned maneuver—the quick directional change—will burn up more energy.
Situation 2—The ball hits the left wall, then the back wall, and finally bounces into the middle of backcourt. Make the shot with your backhand.

This situation is identical to the first, except that the ball may be moving more slowly because it has hit more walls and is closer to centercourt. Your options are the same as in Situation 1 except that you can use a clever ploy—fake a drive down the left wall and hit a backhand reverse pinch into the right corner.

This shot is designed to pin your opponent to the right wall, keeping him from getting too much of a head start to the left when the situation arises again. If he moves too far to the left, you can hit the same reverse pinch, but behind

SIDE-WALL FOOTWORK AND BODYWORK
In this series of photos, follow the action from top to bottom on this page and then from top to bottom on the next page. The sequence illustrates the type of footwork and bodywork you need to make shots near a side wall deep in backcourt.

his back. In either case, he won't return your shot unless it comes off the left wall because you've taken his running start away from him.

Situation 3—The ball comes directly off the back wall. Should you hit a forehand or backhand? You should use the shot that is substantially better than the other. If you have a super forehand and a so-so backhand, use the forehand. But if neither one is far superior to the other, choose the one that places your body between the ball and your opponent. This maneuver opens up a greater scoring lane, especially if you allow yourself a few extra steps to step into the ball.

On a floater to the back wall, the advanced player will "hook" his opponent with his body. In this maneuver, he plants himself in centercourt and waits for his opponent to decide on a defensive position. As his opponent begins to move, he moves with him, with his back toward his opponent, forcing his opponent to move even farther to the side of the court, away from the coverage zone.

Situation 4—The ball bounces to the back wall, but you don't have time or room to take a full swing. Should you hit it into the back wall, hoping it will reach the front wall? Most players will elect to do so. But you should avoid this shot unless there is absolutely no other alternative. When an advanced player sees someone hitting a ball into the back wall, he will rush the front wall and softly volley the ball low after it comes off the front wall. This leaves you stuck in backcourt.

If possible, get your racquet behind the ball and push up a half-lob. Although an advanced player may still try to volley the ball, he has much less time to do so. Furthermore, if your lob is reasonably deep, you will force him out of centercourt, giving you time to recover and assume a good defensive position.

Summary—The court maneuvers in the first three situations are possible because according to the rules you *must be given an unobstructed approach to the ball.* They constitute what I call bodywork and, like footwork, are indispensable skills for improving your chances for scoring.

When practicing footwork you strive to get the "feel" of the court. When practicing shot-making, you strive to get the "feel" of the racquet. When practicing bodywork, you strive to get the "feel" of your opponent.

CHAPTER THIRTEEN

Other Shots

Although I have covered all of the shots necessary for playing winning racquetball, there are numerous other shots. Most of them are of limited use at the advanced level either because they have strong countershots or because there are better alternatives.

However, some of them are useful, even at the advanced level, as an occasional surprise. These other shots are the Z ball, around-the-wall ball, drop shot and overhead (drive and kill).

Z BALL

The *Z ball* is like the Z serve except that it hits a second side wall before bouncing on the floor. A perfect Z ball hits the side wall about a foot or two from the back wall and travels almost parallel to the back wall.

But nobody hits a perfect Z ball consistently. Furthermore, the shot spends so much time in the air that you can almost walk to the coverage zone in backcourt. Finally, the shot is a setup unless hit perfectly because it travels so slowly after hitting two side walls.

However, the Z ball is a difficult shot for most beginners to return because it is a side-wall shot that can take bizarre bounces. But once a player realizes that he should position himself deep on the side of the court opposite the second side wall of the Z ball, it is an easy shot to kill.

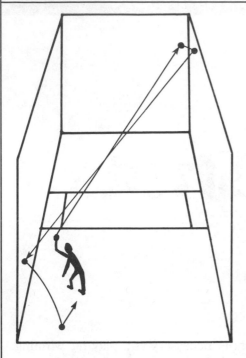

A Z ball made with a backhand stroke can look like this.

AROUND-THE-WALL BALL

The *around-the-wall ball* is like the Z ball except that it strikes a side wall first—about 10 to 15 feet high. Then it hits the front wall, the other side wall and finally the floor. This shot is even less useful than the Z ball.

If the around-the-wall ball looks like it will go through centercourt, step up and volley the ball to end the rally. By cutting off the ball, you can take almost any shot because your opponent is trapped behind you in backcourt. You also don't have to contend with the strange bounces that occur when you let the ball bounce.

Although you might not end the rally, you will put your opponent on the defensive. If the ball is deep, treat it as you would a Z ball. Position yourself deep in backcourt.

DROP SHOT

The classic *drop shot* is another shot with limited usefulness. It is a soft, stiff-wristed shot, hit with some underspin. The ball is usually directed into one of the front corners. It is a tough shot to control. A small error in the stroke makes it a setup for your opponent.

Furthermore, it travels so slowly to the front wall that any alert player can

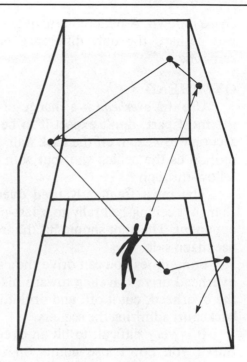

The around-the-wall ball hits a side wall first.

When having to return an around-the-wall ball, consider cutting it off and volleying it for a winner.

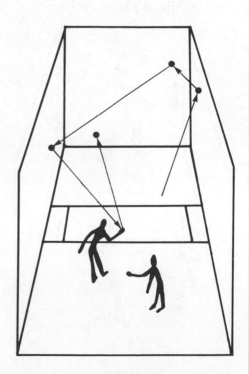

chase it down. A better alternative is to firmly punch the ball into a front corner. But perhaps the only difference between a drop shot and a firm punch is semantic.

OVERHEAD

Use the *overhead* as a change-of-pace alternative to the ceiling shot. But for the most part, don't expect it to be a consistent winner. Also, it requires fine accuracy to keep it off the back wall. You hit it with the same overhand throwing motion as the ceiling shot but with an added downward snap of the wrist and follow-through.

The most frequently used overhead is the *overhead drive*. You use it to change a ceiling-ball rally to a fast-paced series of ground strokes or to jam an opponent. The shot should hit the front wall about two to four feet high on the backhand side.

Sometimes you can drive the ball past a lazy opponent or jam him with an overhead drive traveling toward his shoulder. But an alert player will step into the overhead, cut it off, and drill it into a front corner, leaving you standing in backcourt admiring the scenery.

It is very difficult to hit an overhead that doesn't come off the back wall. But if you don't lose points on more than 50% of your tries, it may be worthwhile as a surprise shot.

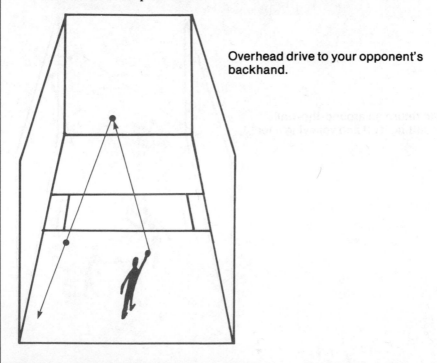

Overhead drive to your opponent's backhand.

The *overhead kill* is just a kill from an overhead, usually directed from a backcourt corner into the opposite forecourt corner. This shot is even harder to hit than the overhead drive because it must be hit low and soft enough to not come off a side wall. But any ball angled down from six to seven feet high will take a high bounce off the floor, no matter how low on the front wall you hit it.

If you can develop a consistent overhead kill, use it during ceiling-shot rallies when your opponent is standing next to you in backcourt or when he is loafing.

To defend against the overhead kill, you must always watch your opponent. If he snaps his wrist downward from over his head, take off quickly for the forecourt coverage zone. You don't need to watch the ball travel to the front wall. It will appear in the coverage zone when you get there. If you get there on time, your opponent will be too far away to return your low tap into the front wall.

There are numerous other shots of even less usefulness than those discussed here. I strongly suggest that you spend your time perfecting the bread-and-butter shots before spending any time on the shots described here. They are fun to practice as a change-of-pace and may help you improve your options. But generally they have limited use in real-game situations. This is especially true at advanced levels.

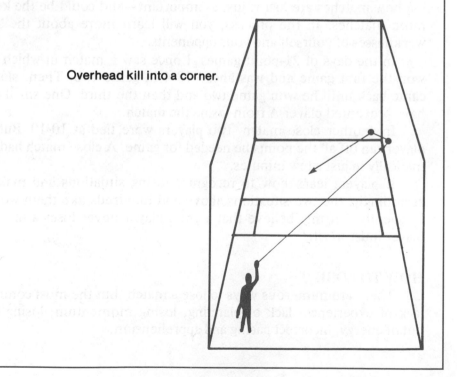

Overhead kill into a corner.

CHAPTER FOURTEEN

How Matches Are Lost

When giving pointers on strategy, racquetball instructors usually emphasize how matches are won. They seldom discuss how matches are lost. Understanding how matches are lost is just as important—and could be the key to winning more matches. In the process, you will learn more about the strengths and weaknesses of yourself and your opponents.

In the days of 21-point games, I once saw a match in which player A had won the first game and was ahead 18-4 in game two. Then, slowly, player B came back until he won game two and then the third. One small change might have prevented player A from losing the match.

In another close match, two players were tied at 10-10. But quickly, one player ran off all the points he needed for game. A close match had changed dramatically in just a few minutes.

If players learn how to recognize losing situations and make corrections accordingly, the two situations above and hundreds like them would occur less frequently. I firmly believe that a great player never loses a match. The other player must *win* it.

HOW TO LOSE

There are numerous ways to lose a match, but the most common deal with lack of experience, lack of planning, losing momentum, losing cool, running out of energy, incorrect pacing and apprehension.

Seldom is the situation as bleak as it appears. There often is a key step that will get you out of the difficulty you are in. You just have to know where to look and what to expect. Of course, top players have looked into those places and mentally recorded what they've seen. But it takes many, many hours of on-court experience to get where they are.

I will share some of these insights with you, but in the end you still have to do your own looking. You must interpret what you see in terms of your own abilities and the abilities of your opponent.

In the following situations, you can substitute the words *match play* for *tournament* if you do not play tournaments. Match play is any match played for anything other than recreation.

LACK OF TOURNAMENT EXPERIENCE

Perhaps you lack tournament experience. You can play in 100 tournaments a year and still, in a sense, lack tournament experience. This applies to practice matches as well. You have to consider the quality of the tournaments you enter. If every tournament is a breeze, and you stay in your own little niche, the first tough tournament will probably make you feel like a novice. In fact, it could be worse for you because you might not be able to cope with pressure from unfamiliar shot patterns, rules and opponents.

A tournament adds a new dimension to your game because you try your best. And your opponent is going to do everything he can to keep you from winning. As competition increases, the shots, psychological ploys and game situations presented will be more diverse.

I suggest that you plan your tournament schedule to expose yourself progressively to better and better competition one step at a time. This means finding a comfortable level of tournament competition. Play at it while occasionally signing up for tougher tournaments.

This approach also applies to practice matches. But don't choose competition totally out of your league because you won't gain anything except discouragement.

LACK OF VARIED EXPERIENCES

I've heard many players say, "I just got destroyed. I couldn't get my timing." This often happens at the local level. Players play at one club with the same kind of ball and the same racquet week after week. They spend a lot of time picking just the right ball and sometimes haggle with the court attendant about not getting their favorite court.

They don't realize that what they've done is practice under conditions almost entirely different from what they will encounter in match play. Not only that, but they haven't learned to adjust to a different environment. I won't say that you should go out of your way to find the worst playing conditions possible, but you certainly shouldn't be too picky about conditions either.

About two weeks before a tournament, start playing with the tournament ball. But even then you may not be reproducing the tournament conditions. Changes in court surface, lighting and humidity can also have a dramatic effect on play. Reduce as many variables as you can. If possible, play a few games on different tournament courts a day or two before the tournament. But don't be surprised if the courts still seem different during the tournament. When 200 players gather around they can produce a lot of body heat! That *will* change playing conditions.

Finally, use at least two racquets interchangeably instead of sticking to one favorite racquet. I've seen players go from hot to cold after breaking the strings or frame of a favorite racquet. They seem to have no confidence with another racquet. Do make sure that the grips are similar. This feel is most important.

When you finally get on the court to warm up for your match, remember the priorities previously described—weight shift, wrist snap and shot flexibility. Work on these aspects of the stroke during warmup to get your shot range tuned to court conditions. By the end of the warmup, you should be able to "feel" the court and ball. Don't forget to practice hitting some quick exchange shots to warm up your reflexes.

NO GAME PLAN

Another "loser" is the player with no game plan. He is never sure why he lost. During a match you should be able to figure out your opponent's best and worst shots, his best and worst serves, his type of game (power or control), his degree of shot flexibility, his speed and endurance, and his maturity.

Your initial game plan should include setting up situations that test your assumptions about the player's style of play. If those assumptions are correct, go to part two of the plan—attack him at his most vulnerable spots. If the assumptions are wrong and you have found different vulnerable spots, adjust the plan accordingly and carry out a different attack. There is no time to originate a complete game plan during the course of a match.

Players who go into a match without a game plan are easy to spot. They are apprehensive and never mount a serious attack. Most likely, the match is very short because their opponents do have a game plan. They find and attack weak spots immediately.

COASTING

This is letting up when you are ahead. I know all about it because it is perhaps my greatest foible. It happens to all of us. When you're up by 10 points, it's tough to grit your teeth and play 100%. When you coast, you don't usually lose the match in a rainstorm of kill shots. You are more likely to see your big lead erode slowly.

Most players with big leads figure that all they have to do is get a few lousy points. So why worry? But once you lose your momentum, it's tough to get it back. Even if you are lucky enough to get the needed few points, you'll probably lose the next game because you've stopped scoring.

This is definitely not the time to play defensively. You must play *more* aggressively. Perhaps change the pattern of play by cutting off lob serves, shooting drive serves, and so forth—anything to change the tempo of the game and get more aggressive.

Don't start this when the game is almost over, but much earlier. Even if you lose the game, your aggressive play can carry through to the next, allowing you to regain momentum. If you had a huge lead, you probably are the better player anyway. You must reestablish this in your opponent's mind and regain your offensive game.

LOSING YOUR COOL

The most dramatic way to lose a match is by losing your cool and going into an *uncontrollable* rage. The controllable kind is OK. The master of the controllable rage was Charlie Brumfield. He would go into a rage whenever he got far behind. His opponent would quit with a whimper because he didn't want to have anything to do with a madman. Or he'd go into an uncontrollable rage himself because he would get flustered by all the shouting.

When you go out of control, your face flushes, your heartbeat increases, and you tend to scream unintelligible nonsense at the crowd, the referee and your opponent.

Ideally, you should play without inner emotion. You must keep control of yourself and your surroundings during a match. If you lose that control, you can lose 10 or 15 points in a matter of minutes. Your judgment becomes impaired and you can't make quick decisions anymore.

When a bad call goes against you, make it known that you think it is a bad call. But accept it as just something that happens during the course of a match. You cannot dwell on one little instance. In club play, the solution is to stop playing people who make a lot of bad calls.

In a tournament, if the number of bad calls gets to be more than three, I look for a new referee or linesman. But there's no reason to go berserk. If you like to entertain the crowd and you know that you won't get ejected from the match, go into a controlled rage and blow off steam. But you'd better be a good actor and a congenial person. Otherwise, you'll get a bad reputation.

RUNNING OUT OF ENERGY

Racquetball would be easy if matches were painless. But everyone runs out of energy at one time or another. It might happen because you're out of condition or nervous. Or you might be in a marathon match lasting two or three hours. Whatever the reason, the worst response is to change the entire game to passing shots and defense.

Try some ceiling shots to slow the pace until you can get your second wind. Use lob serves and take as much time as legally possible between points.

Stay away from passing shots as much as possible, especially crosscourt shots. Although it may seem safer to go to crosscourt passing shots giving a greater margin for error, you are only prolonging your eventual defeat. Crosscourts will make you run more.

Once you catch your breath with a few ceiling-ball rallies, start looking for kill-shot opportunities. Use them to end the rally as soon as possible.

If you still have enough strength, hit some drive serves. If your opponent is as tired as you, you should be able to get some quick, easy aces or winners. Vary your serves and shots, but always try to be on the offensive. You want to avoid long rallies.

At this point in the match, one of you will probably hit the same "wall" that marathon runners hit when they just can't deliver any more energy to their muscles. Hitting crosscourt passing shots only increases your chance of hitting this wall. You should hit shots that make your opponent bend down as much as possible. If he's tired, even if he gets to the ball, he will not hit an effective shot. Don't prolong the match. Go for the kill.

GIVING UP

Another way to lose is to assume that there's no way you can win. This tends to occur when your opponent is hitting every shot in the book, and you're just chasing the ball. In this case, try to determine why you are being outgunned. It may be that you are too apprehensive and defensive in your shot selection. Or, perhaps you haven't tried all avenues of attack.

I've seen matches in which one player hopelessly behind suddenly finds the other player's weakness. I once saw a player win by hitting 10 Z serves in a row to the forehand after he found that his opponent couldn't handle the serve.

Hitting to the ceiling slows down the game to give you time to think and recover. However, if you decide that your opponent is way out of your league, go for broke. Ceiling shots and passing shots won't do anything but eventually produce setups for your opponent. Hit enough ceiling and passing shots to allow yourself time to set up. But then go for the winner as soon as possible. If you lose, you lose. But at least you tried the only game plan that had a chance of winning.

TRYING TOO HARD

It *is* possible to try too hard. For example, you may want to beat someone so badly that you overhit the ball or sprint after balls that you could reach with a casual run.

To perform your best, you must be relaxed. A little nervousness is often a good sign that adrenalin is flowing and you are alert. But too much nervous energy drains you. The only cure for this is to get experience playing different people. Adopt the view that there is no such thing as a do-or-die match. Again, play with controlled emotions.

APPREHENSION

Another frequent cause for losing a match is apprehension. There can be many reasons for this. I've mentioned some already. But whatever the cause, there is only one way to get out of the doldrums—play all out. Change your shot patterns and attack the ball. For example, cut off all soft serves either by making volleys or half-volleys. Try a power game. Shake your opponent's concentration.

Even if you don't make a bunch of winners, you'll force your opponent to change his game plan and shot selection. In this new situation, you might find that you are now outgunning him. Or, if you return to your original game plan, you may find that your opponent can't find the same rhythm he once had.

Hit harder and lower. What you may find is that you were pushing or killing the ball from knee high instead of ankle high. Hitting all out will loosen you up.

SUMMARY

As helpful as the suggested remedies may be, they cannot be learned in the heat of a serious match. They must be instinctive by the time you step onto the court. That's why you must try these responses in practice sessions. If it is not possible, you may be playing practice matches that are too easy. Move up to some tougher competition once in a while. A practice match is the time to experiment.

Whenever you lose, ask yourself why. Think of things to try differently the next time. Build up a storehouse of potential avenues of attack. Only this way can you acquire the experience to turn your game around during a match.

CHAPTER FIFTEEN

Improving Your Game

A neophyte struggles with basic strokes, angles, and the frustrations of failure. The intermediate grapples with the complexities of a game he once thought was within reach of mastering. The advanced player dreams not just of refining shots and strategies but of unlocking secrets that can make his play brilliant. The fact is that we all want to improve our game one way or another.

Previous chapters are packed with tips and specific drills for improving your game. This chapter takes a more general approach. It discusses some do's and don'ts for improving your game and tells you how you can learn from watching other players.

KNOW YOUR GOALS

A player without a plan is like a rower without a paddle. Neither determines his own destination. He wanders from year to year without accomplishing any significant goals. You should ask yourself what you want out of racquetball in a year, in five years, and so forth. When defining your goals, be realistic. Not everyone can become a champion in two years.

Once you identify the main goal, consider those skills and strategies that will help you achieve it. Then devise a realistic plan. For example, you might spend one month concentrating on the forehand, another month on the backhand, and so forth. The plan may be not work perfectly, but have a plan anyway. Only then can you make adjustments. Write down the plan so you can refer to it occasionally. Evaluate your progress and reevaluate your plan. A racquetball diary serves this purpose. In addition to recording your goals, keep a record of your play and practice. Be honest!

KNOW YOURSELF

You should get an understanding of your strengths and weaknesses. Shape your offense around your strengths. Plan practice sessions around your weaknesses.

Choose a strategy that fits your personality. For example, if you are the quiet, analytic type, choose a control-oriented offense and practice evaluation techniques that give results you can analyze. But if you are a go-getter who has trouble sitting still, choose a serve-and-shoot offense.

Try to rank the different aspects of your game with respect to those you play. Know when you should go for the kill and when you should defend. By understanding the quality of your skills, you can properly select the right shots and strategies. This way you use your strengths to their utmost and make as few errors as possible. Basically, your opponents must earn every point they win.

To understand your skills relative to your opponent's, determine your *scoring zones.* These are court areas where you can make shots with about a 90% success rate. Compare your scoring zones with your opponent's.

Have your club pro or a knowledgeable friend count your success ratio—number of successes divided by number of tries—for various shots in a match-play situation.

Video equipment can also help you understand your game. Videotape your practice sessions and your matches. Then critically review them yourself, with other players, or a club pro. You can also record other players and compare. Sometimes, glaring differences are immediately obvious.

On defensive shots, strive to move the ball into your most productive scoring zones. For example, my best scoring zone is any place on my backhand side. Because my backhand is better than anyone else's backhand, and because I am strong, I'll go for a kill shot from deep-left court even when my opponent is in centercourt. The velocity and accuracy of my backhand makes the shot worthwhile for me.

BE CREATIVE

Rules of thumb, principles, and techniques should never be viewed as rigid and absolute. What is unorthodox today may be common practice later—and vice-versa. Who would have dreamed that I could build an entire strategy around power and the pendulum swing?

Try to remain mentally flexible. Occasionally reevaluate the basics of shot-making and strategy. In the process, you may find new relationships and insights that allow you to improve your game.

Be creative during match play. Although I have said, "This shot is use-less..." and "This strategy should be avoided...," there are exceptions to every rule. Stick with sound principles during the progress of a match, but also be alert to situations where the exception applies.

EXPERIMENT

Try new shots and new techniques. Not only do they keep your creative juices flowing, but they help you develop a feel for shots. Time spent practicing techniques that don't work is not wasted. It gives you a broader perspective of the useful shots.

There are also times when a new idea doesn't work on the first try. The pieces may fall together on a second or third try.

PRACTICE MAKES PERFECT (SOMETIMES)

There is an art to practicing shots and strategies. I suggest the adage "If at first you don't succeed, try again." Many people interpret this to mean that if you don't succeed, just try harder and you will eventually succeed. But such an attitude can be counterproductive.

Trying harder conveys an image of gritting your teeth and spending more time working on a particular shot. But, in fact, trying again really implies practicing and executing good habits. Shots must come naturally to be effective under game conditions.

Moreover, the longer you work at any shot without a break, the more likely you will reinforce bad habits. The best approach to improving a shot is to spend a few quality, 30-minute sessions trying to work out problems. If it still isn't right, go on to something else and come back to it a few days or weeks later.

Visualization—I've found that if I take time off and play other sports, I actually improve some of my shots without even stepping on the court. Some people would attribute the improvement to latent learning, others to the complementary skills gained from playing other sports. I think there's some truth to these theories, but I also think that some improvement was gained through *visualization*.

I replay rallies and shots in my head, more so during the off-season when I am not contending with the drudgeries of tournament preparation. On-court adjustments and experimentation take a tremendous amount of time and energy. But shots can be replayed and adjusted instantly in your mind.

Sometimes I am even able to remember the feel or sensation of the shot during my mental practice sessions. Therefore, standing on a court and hitting a shot 1000 times is not always the answer to improving a particular shot.

CONCENTRATE WHILE PLAYING

Bringing your non-racquetball life onto the court with you is a lot of extra baggage to carry around. Leave those burdens outside the court and focus your attention on playing good racquetball. Sharpen your concentration by watching your opponent's wrist snap, footwork and bodywork. Stick with a simple strategy and hit well with good follow-through.

Steve Garvey on Mental Alertness

Maintaining a high level of concentration throughout a match isn't always easy. Adopting an offensive strategy will help your concentration. Watching for *visual keys* helps me stay alert. These are motions, foot placement, or some other part of stroke production that gives away your opponent's intentions.

Avoid burn-out. If playing becomes a chore, do something else for a few weeks. Most people play better after a vacation. Keep fit by participating in other sports. You may be a little disoriented during the first few minutes back on the court, but the feeling will go away if you warm up slowly and concentrate on having fun and moving your feet.

DIVERSIFY YOUR PLAYING SCHEDULE

Don't play the same person day in and day out. You will improve much more slowly because you know what he will do from memory. Play a good mix of styles and ability levels. Variety gives you the range of experiences necessary to quickly respond to changing situations. Keep the game interesting.

Play slightly better players to provide the challenge that heightens your competitive spirit and exposes weaknesses. But avoid getting in over your head. You gain nothing by playing a far superior player. And you just waste his time.

Also play slightly worse players. This will help you restore confidence and practice new shots and strategies without always being pressured. However, avoid players who are so bad that they won't do anything for your game.

PRACTICE PATTERNS

Every player should devote a portion of his practice time to *patterns*. These develop the "muscle memory" necessary for instinctive reactions during match play. They also make the best use of your practice time for developing footwork, control and stamina.

Furthermore, patterns develop the necessary discipline for long matches. Playing patterns is much more physically intensive than playing a match. During matches, a good part of the time is spent retrieving the ball and serving, time that is eliminated while practicing patterns.

There is a different set of practice patterns for each ability level. But they should all:

1) Allow you to sustain long rallies.

2) Occur frequently enough during match play to be useful. It makes no sense for a beginner to practice the two-on-one pattern, in which two players rifle shots at another player. Beginners will return very few of the shots.

Pattern playing should concentrate on one or two shots at a time or on a particular phase of the game. It should allow you to repeat a shot many times in a short period of time. Each shot and its response should be agreed upon in advance by all players. There are only short pauses between rallies.

Patterns for Beginners—Beginners need to concentrate on developing footwork, stamina and consistency. Fancy shot patterns do them no good. They need to develop confidence in their ability to run down every ball bouncing above the knees. Beginners should use slower balls to prolong rallies and give them more time to react and adjust. Enough rest periods help keep players alert.

Here are some example patterns for beginners:

1) Both players stand in the left-rear zone. Player A initiates the rally by hitting the ball into the right side of the court but away from the right wall.

Player B chases the ball and hits a forehand into the right half of the court but away from the right wall. Then he circles back to the left-rear zone while player A chases the ball. The objective is to practice the forehand and court movement exclusively.

See how long you can keep the rally going. Concentrate on control and consistency, not power. The same drill can be modified for the backhand.

2) Two players stand in backcourt, one on either side of the court. One player hits crosscourts with his forehand. The other hits crosscourts with his backhand. During the rally, each player bounces on his toes and shuffles into position to hit the ball below his waist.

After hitting each shot, the returner announces the number of shots that have been successfully returned. After 10 minutes, switch sides and repeat the drill. Give the other player a chance to practice both forehand and backhand. This pattern concentrates on making minor adjustments and practicing forehand and backhand with as little movement as possible.

3) After each player is able to sustain long rallies in the other drills, play short practice games—7 or 11 points. Use just one type of serve and hit to the

open court during the rally. The goal is not to see who can win the game, but to keep the ball in play with shots that drive your opponent out of centercourt. Each player should bounce on the balls of his feet and shuffle into position to hit a controlled shot. Each player should move in and out of centercourt.

Patterns for Intermediates—Intermediates can usually move around the court fairly well. To the inexperienced eye they seem to possess all the shots of an advanced player. But they lack consistency and the ability to shoot the ball on the run. They also have other deficiencies that an advanced player can spot and attack.

Patterns for intermediates should improve weaknesses and polish strengths. The goal is an eventual jump to the advanced level. Some examples of patterns for intermediates follow:

1) Both players stand in backcourt and trade forehand ceiling shots up centercourt. The objective is to see how long you can continue the rally. After 5 or 10 minutes, repeat the drill with the backhand ceiling shot.

Then move closer to the left wall and repeat the drill. Once you can keep the rally going for 25 or 50 shots, place a mark on the centercourt spot and repeat the drill. Now, a player must move up to the mark after hitting the ceiling shot. This variation increases the degree of difficulty and is guaranteed to get your heart pumping.

2) This drill is designed for developing a consistent crosscourt shot. Play begins with player A standing in centercourt with the ball and player B in backcourt. Player A taps a setup to one of the rear corners. Player B drives player A out of centercourt with a crosscourt and moves into centercourt.

Then player A drives player B out of centercourt with a crosscourt. Because each player knows what the other will hit, the rally lasts longer than normal. Each player gets more time to set up for each shot.

3) Begin as in pattern 2, but this time each player must hit a crosscourt from backcourt and a down-the-wall from centercourt or forecourt. The ceiling is off limits. An obvious variation of this pattern drill is to substitute a near-side pinch for the down-the-wall.

4) This pattern drill is best performed with three players, one being the ball boy who clears the floor of stray balls. The second player is the feeder who stands in the left-rear zone and hits short crosscourts to the right side of the court. The third person is the shooter who positions himself in centercourt and cuts off the crosscourt with a forehand kill down-the-wall.

The ball boy runs after the balls and places them in a bucket he carries. The shooter moves quickly back to his centercourt position after each shot. The feeder hits another crosscourt as soon as the shooter reaches his centercourt position, brings his racquet up above his waist and announces how many shots he has taken. After 25 shots, players change roles.

5) Play short games—7 or 11 points—using the patterns described. Allow only one type of serve and a limited number of patterns.

Patterns for Advanced and Championship Players—Advanced players have no major weaknesses. They know how to attack all weaknesses. They can score from anywhere and at anytime, even under adverse conditions.

Separating the championship player from the advanced player is a matter of degree and commitment. For the championship player, brilliant shot-making is commonplace. Physical and mental toughness have been forged by thousands of hours of grueling practice sessions and tournaments. These upper-echelon players know that only inches and split-seconds separate the winners from the losers.

Practice patterns for intermediates also work for top players. Practice sessions are more strenuous merely because their defenses are better. But additional patterns must be added to meet special needs. Rallies at this level often require super-quick reflexes. Offensive opportunities appear for only a split-second. No offensive opportunity can be bypassed for fear that it may not appear again.

The two-on-one technique works in all of the pattern drills to sharpen reflexes and to place greater stress on a player. In this technique, two players play against one. The single player must execute the patterns against the other two players. Because two players can cover more court, their returns will come quickly and accurately. This technique simulates the frenzied rally that occurs when a player is pressed by another on a hot streak, or makes a mistake and then must recover.

Summary—Practicing patterns is the most efficient technique for improving your game. Combine them with solitary sessions where you have time to sort out the wrinkles in your shots.

LESSONS

Lessons improve your game by providing you with someone who objectively evaluates your strengths and weaknesses. Even championship players will go to a coach for advice when they suspect that an adjustment is necessary for improvement.

Find someone who has a good reputation for teaching other players with your ability. Then take a lesson to see if you feel comfortable with him.

Each teaching pro has a slightly different view of what's right. Use him as a source of information. Try to integrate what he tells you with your view of racquetball. The best teaching pros can adapt to your philosophy if it has merit. They will convince you to change it if it doesn't.

If you are an advanced player, you will find that there are few teaching pros who can meet your needs. That's because unless they have played at your level, they can't understand your game. You have to learn by evaluating what you hear and read from top players.

WATCH GOOD PLAYERS

Careful watching of a good match between two top players can sometimes do as much for your game as months of practice. Think of it as a silent instructional. The players have the techniques and strategies that go into winning racquetball.

Trying to learn a shot-making technique from words alone is almost impossible. Pictures help. But watching it live or on film is the best way. Not only will you see how shots are made, but you will see variations.

There is no one exact method for hitting a forehand. Each player hits it differently. But better players demonstrate the basic fundamentals in their strokes more often than others. Seeing various techniques improves your chances of finding someone whose methods you can copy.

While watching top players, try to relate the principles and ideas in this book to what is happening on the court. How does a top player hit the ball with so much power yet with apparently little energy? Why is it that he seems to never move out of centercourt? What shots does he use to score most of his points? What service strategy is he using? What are his most effective service-return strategies?

Finding the answers to these questions may crystallize the ideas that you've read about in this book and heard in the locker room.

A match between top players is great entertainment, but the perceptive spectator comes away from the match with much more. He picks up subtle shifts in strategy, the finer points of making a particular shot, tactical and stylistic differences between the players, and so forth.

In making the jump from intermediate to advanced player, you have to rely partly on observation and analysis for improvement. There is a small circle of players who understand enough about the game to help you with yours. Although many top players may share some of their knowledge with you while you are an intermediate, few will help you when you get within striking distance of them.

Plotting the course of a champion would be educational. A champion, whether at the local or national level, has proven through consistency, tenacity and resilience that he deserves to be a champion. He always finds out why he lost and subsequently finds a way to win again.

SCOUT YOUR OPPONENTS

Analyzing your opponent's strengths and weaknesses may do more to improve your score than your game. But something can be learned from watching anyone, even the lowly novice. Scouting allows you to enter a court with a game plan.

There's no sense in working harder than you have to. If a player can't return a Z serve, you should know about it before the match starts. Some of the general things to evaluate in your opponent are speed, reflexes, height, playing style, mental control and physical endurance.

For each player category there is a standard avenue of attack. Some other points to note are the following: What are his responses to different serves? What are his favorite serves? How effective are they? Does he telegraph them? Watch his service motion to pick up signals you can use.

If you can't scout your opponent, see if you can get a trusted friend to scout him for you. Even if you watch your opponent play, it's good to get a second opinion. The worst thing to do is to go onto a court not knowing what you're going to do.

The second worst thing to do is to go into a match with a rigid game plan that you won't change. Instead, start with a well-defined plan based on your scouting report.

During the beginning phase of the match—the first five points—test your plan. See if his weaknesses are still there. As the match progresses, constantly reevaluate the plan and adapt it to the situation. This is the hard part because you have to make a judgment about your abilities. Ideally, the plan gels as the match progresses.

Learning is never over. A new shot, a cunning ploy, a revolutionary strategy is always available. Remember that success is the result of many small steps—some forward and some backward—but always one at a time. Don't try to do too much at once. If you have a string of failures, lower your expectations. Give yourself a chance to succeed. When success comes easily, raise your goals. Only then can you experience the thrill of athletic rewards.

CHAPTER SIXTEEN

Becoming An Advanced Player

If you've read all the preceding chapters, you've received a lot of information. Now you've reached a point where you can continue on your own. I have covered all of the shots, strategies and techniques necessary to play winning racquetball. It is now up to you to understand, analyze and apply the ideas.

The remainder of this book takes a peek at racquetball at the championship level. It is not intended to be complete but only a sampler of serves, shots and tournament preparation. These chapters give you a glimpse of where you might be in the near future. You'll find some ideas that you can probably use right away.

To understand championship racquetball—and the modern game—you must understand the basic tenets of the power game. The era of the pure power game has now evolved into a combination of power and control. Analyzing the pure power game reveals the on-court struggles that occur at the championship level as contrasting styles battle for supremacy.

THE POWER GAME

As the founder and head disciple of the serve-and-shoot style of play, I have become synonomous with the phrase *power game*. But in truth, the words are misleading because they imply undisciplined, unthinking ball-blasting. Nothing is further from the truth. A better term is perhaps *power-based* racquetball. But because very few people use that phrase, I drop *-based*.

I created my power game at the St. Louis Jewish Community Centers Association when the rest of the world was following the pure *control game*. When I first started playing, I didn't go up into the mountains, meditate for 10 days, and come back with power racquetball. I didn't start with a grand plan. I developed it through long hours of experimentation. I started as a ball blaster, but my game evolved and matured.

In simple terms, power racquetball is a strategy using power as the primary element in winning points, games and matches. In control strategy, power is secondary to accuracy and shot selection. The main difference is emphasis. Your chances of winning diminish if you overemphasize one element at the expense of others.

Basic elements of winning racquetball fall into two groups. In one group are desire, organization, perception, creativity and inner strength. You can't teach people how to acquire these. You either have them or you don't. In the second group are power, accuracy (control), endurance, court coverage and shot selection.

Essentials—Some basic facts of power racquetball follow:

1) Each shot can be less accurate because a mishit can still be missed by your opponent.

2) Shot selection is less critical because your opponent can't effectively counter a ball moving at high speed.

3) Less court space needs to be covered because the ball velocity limits most coverage zones to backcourt.

4) Rallies are short.

In simple terms: If you hit the ball hard enough, you worry less about everything else. Therefore the power player has to decide, "How hard is hard enough?"

That's power racquetball in a nutshell. But let me emphasize that most decisions you make depend on your opponent. That's why no one can continually overemphasize one element and still win.

CLASSIC METHODS

There is no debate on how to win a point: Kill the ball before your opponent does. Even the control player adheres to this rule. The ongoing debate is how to get into a situation where the risk of shooting the ball makes the choice worthwhile.

When a control player plays a power player, he's hoping that the power player will:

1) Get arm fatigue before the end of the match.

2) Get frustrated by a slow pace and high balls.

3) Have a long slump.

4) Make bad shots.

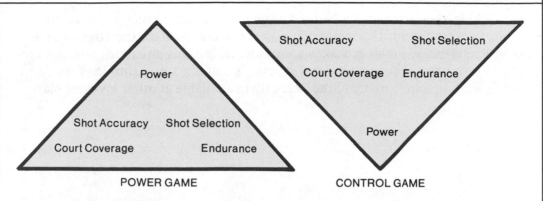

These two triangles indicate the relative emphasis of the elements of racquetball in the power game and control game.

That's why a control player hits to the ceiling, moves the ball side to side, uses high and slow serves, and likes to play with a dead ball.

This archaic strategy still works at the local level. It's fun to see a control player slowly pick apart a power player and reduce him to a beaten, frustrated ball blaster. The control player uses time outs, the wet-floor ploy, and the "would-you-say-the-score-again" trick along with accurate passing shots to reduce the effectiveness of the power player. When the time is right, he shoots more frequently to make the points start rolling in.

At first glance, the control strategy looks foolproof because there's no pressure to be always "on." Just do your leg work and wait for the opposition to make bad shots.

But the game has changed. The basic assumptions of the classic control game are weak at the local level and wrong at higher levels. The power player at the top is so accurate, quick and strong that the classic control game has evolved into control with power in reserve. Everyone at the top has to be able to blow the ball by his opponent when the situation dictates. It may be fun to see a control player pick apart a power player, but it's awesome when a power player destroys a control player.

To beat the power player, the control player has to predict how successful his classic control strategy will be. This depends in part on how far each player has developed his personal style. It also depends on the situation—such as whether the ball is slow or fast. If the control player's prediction comes out negative, there's only one answer left for him—serve, shoot and hope for a lucky day.

At the championship level, you cannot squander offensive opportunities. The ball can move around at blinding speed. Players can run down almost every ball and can score from almost impossible positions.

Taking the step from advanced player to a championship one requires a serious commitment. During match play you are always on the edge of defeat, as well as victory. Small mistakes are costly. Given this situation, you can now see why strategy at the championship level is actually quite simple. Your opponent's skills preclude many of the alternatives available at other levels of play.

CHAPTER SEVENTEEN

Championship Service Strategy

The serve is more important in championship play than at other levels. Advanced players won't tolerate long ceiling rallies. If they see the slightest scoring opportunity, they go for it. In practice, this limits the options available to the server.

HARD DRIVE SERVE

The service strategy in the power racquetball game is surprisingly simple: Hit a hard drive serve to the backhand. Let's assume that you are playing a right-handed player. The preferred serve is a low, hard drive serve angled into the left-rear corner. The second bounce hits the floor near the side wall opposite the receiver's position. If the serve is low enough, the ball bounces twice before reaching the back wall. But it is close enough to the side wall to make the receiver reach a long way. This type of serve is tough to return offensively.

The angle of the drive serve makes it difficult to return. By angling from right to left, the ball moves away from the receiver's backhand. The ball is returnable within a limited region. If the serve is moving at high speed, the chances of a weak return are even greater.

Trying to hit the serve into the left-rear corner has some risks. The worst is when the serve comes off the back wall. This is a setup for your opponent. Another mistake to avoid is hitting a serve that hits high on the side wall. Contrary to popular belief, aiming for the side wall is poor strategy. Any ball hitting a side wall slows down considerably. It then becomes a setup unless the ball jams the receiver or takes a bad bounce.

SERVICE COMBINATIONS

Advanced players should use the *3:1 rule* of service combinations.

Basically, for every three drive serves hit to the left-rear corner, you hit one different strong serve. For example, I may use a drive down the right wall to the right-rear corner, a hard Z serve to the forehand, or a jam serve to the left.

To keep your opponent guessing, hit all of these serves with the same motion as the drive serve to the left-rear corner.

Down the Right—Hit a drive serve down the right wall as you would the drive to the left, except that the contact point is deeper in the stance. The serve should run down the right wall without touching it. The ball should bounce twice before hitting the back wall.

However, as long as the ball is along the right wall it is still OK for it to hit the back wall. A weak return is probable because of the element of surprise. The trick is to disguise the serve and keep your opponent leaning to the left. The drive serve to the right is effective late in the match, when fatigue has dulled the receiver's reaction time.

Some pros use the drive serve to the right because they think they can partially—and legally—screen the serve. But I don't like or depend on that strategy. In most cases, pro players can read it. I think more restrictive service rules will eventually diminish the serve's effectiveness.

Z Serve—Hit the hard Z to the right three or four feet high on the front wall. You want it to touch the right side wall in backcourt after the first bounce. Or, you can hit it about six inches high so it just clears the service line and makes its second bounce near the right wall about 10 or 15 feet in front of the back wall.

The low Z serve is effective against a tired player having trouble moving forward quickly. The low Z complements the drive serve to the left because it moves him to the right *and* forward. Of course, if you mishit the low Z, you've given your opponent a setup.

Jam Serve—After bouncing off the front wall, this serve touches the side wall near the floor. You have to experiment to find the best spot on the side wall because the position of the receiver, the liveliness of the ball and the "bite" of the side wall contribute to the serve's final trajectory.

The result should be a fast serve coming into the receiver's body. You hope that the receiver is anticipating a drive to the left and has started his turn in that direction. When he discovers his poor judgment, he is out of position and forced to backpedal. If the ball doesn't lose much speed to the side wall, the receiver will be jammed.

ADVANCED SERVING TECHNIQUE

The best place to stand when serving is about one step right of center in the service zone. You must be off-center to get the right angle. But this also opens you up to a strong return down the left wall. However, I have found that the benefits of the off-center starting position far outweigh the potential losses.

Most likely, the service motion will carry you almost into centercourt. A single step will get you to the left side, and another step gets you to the side wall. You are not as far out of position as you might think. However, if you serve and stand still, you can lose the rally from a mediocre return.

Returning the Return—After every serve, I look for and expect an offensive opportunity. I look for an attempted kill or pass down the left wall. The drive serve to the left moves far enough from my opponent's backhand to make a passing shot unlikely or weak at best. If the return is a ceiling ball, I still have time to recover and return it with another ceiling ball.

The most frequent weak return I get from the drive serve to the left touches the left wall and comes out toward centercourt. When this happens, the receiver is trapped in backcourt. Then I pinch the shot into the left corner.

Practicing the Serve—There's no secret to executing the drive serve. It's a normal forehand power stroke. The contact point is slightly in front of the right hip and about five inches off the ground. Take a full pendulum swing. Hit the ball almost flat with lots of wrist snap.

Experiment with different contact points and weight distribution until the

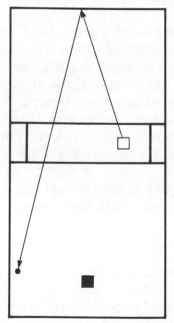

If you are an advanced player, your most effective serve should be a drive to your opponent's backhand.

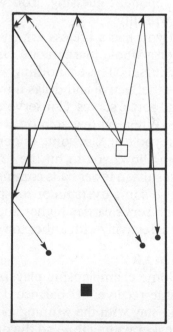

You should also have some surprise serves, such as (1) a drive to the forehand, (2) a hard Z to the forehand and (3) a "jam" serve.

serve acts as you want. Then repeat the shot until it feels smooth and effortless. This "feeling" practice will do more for you at the championship level than counting the number of times that you hit a spot on the front wall.

You should practice the drive serve and its complementary serves for many hours. To implement the 3:1 rule, you need to make the service motion natural, effortless, and seemingly identical for all power serves. At the beginning of the season, I spend many hours practicing drive-serve combinations in hopes of regaining what I lose during summer months of less competitive playing.

Even without the array of complementary serves, the drive serve to the left still offers plenty of opportunities. Many times I have gone into the tie-breaker with nothing to depend on but the drive serve. At those times, I have won more often than not because I hit an effective drive serve. I think this is because I practice it more than any other playing professional.

REFINEMENTS

When the drive serve is working, consider varying delivery speed. This will upset the receiver's timing. Receivers tend to learn when to lean and move if the serve is the same speed every time. By varying delivery speed, you can keep your opponent guessing. You want to create insecurity and bad balance. His game will suffer.

If you had a tireless arm, you could then hit the drive serve using the 3:1 rule for a whole tournament. Unfortunately, *no one* is that strong. You have to pace yourself. There's nothing worse than being so tired that the drive serve becomes ineffective and drags down your game. When necessary, use more junk, lob and soft Z serves. Conserve enough energy for an entire tournament.

Spin—When putting spin on a serve, don't exaggerate the motion. Disguise it as best you can. Use some underspin when hitting junk or soft Z serves. The underspin allows you to hit the serve deeper without losing control of the serve. This results in fewer balls coming off the back wall.

Use some overspin or topspin when hitting junk or high-lob serves. A topspin lob serve carries higher and deeper than normal. Thus, the junk serve can be hit effectively with either top or underspin.

SUMMARY

Some championship players say that you should continually vary serves to keep the receiver off balance. I disagree. Once the drive serve is working, you should stay with the winning game plan. If a player has a weakness, it will only get weaker with time. And the drive serve will reveal it.

The power game revolves around the drive serve. Master it and you will have much of the game wrapped up.

Action Gallery

Harnett chases a down-the-wall shot from McCoy.

Dave Peck making a crosscourt forehand.

Williams and Wright battling for centercourt.

Sometimes you have to do unorthodox things to avoid a hinder call, such as in this Mike Yellen/Charlie Brumfield match.

As Harnett returns a shot, Ed Andrews starts moving toward the ball's destination.

Hillecher's backhand form doesn't seem to bother Mike Yellen. He's watching the ball!

When your opponent is down, go for the kill.

Winning a national championship makes all of the effort worthwhile.

CHAPTER EIGHTEEN

Championship Shot-Making

The apparent superiority of the championship player over the rest of the pack lies in his ability to score from nonideal positions. The modern forehand and backhand shots work great when a player doesn't have time to set up for a picture-perfect shot.

Such situations occur when you are jammed against the side wall, in the middle of a centercourt slugout, in pursuit of the ball on a dead run or when the ball takes a bad bounce. Most players in these situations barely hit the ball back. They rarely turn the tables. But championship players do better than that. They go for a rapid shot and try for a winner.

Take a look at the difference between the modern pendulum swing and the classic "straight-back" swing. You can execute the modern stroke while standing almost straight up—or falling backwards if need be. This gives you an advantage in midcourt play. While your opponent must punch or block his shots, you can hit any shot quickly and with confidence. The modern windup gives you an edge because you can always be on the offensive. Moreover, you can hit effortlessly.

One common, nonideal position occurs when a ball comes directly at you off the front wall, leaving you with no time to move. You can still shoot from this open stance by using the modern swing. The main ideas can be illustrated with the forehand. They apply as well to the backhand or when the ball must be volleyed or half-volleyed.

BASIC PRINCIPLES

There are four main factors involved in hitting a quick, open-stance forehand: flexible wrist action, good contact point, whip-like arm motion and controlled weight transfer.

Flexible wrist action is the most important part of the shot. If necessary, you can drive or kill a normal shot with a moderately stiff wrist. But there's no way you can react fast enough to a fast ball with a slow, stiff wrist action. You need the wrist to adjust timing or to generate power when you can't transfer weight toward the target area.

The contact point can be much deeper than called for in the classic forehand. In fact, you can hit a quick forehand with lots of pace even when the ball is behind your body. Because the contact point is deep in the stance, you will have more time to react to the ball than in a more classic shot. You also need to learn how to react to the ball with one continuous arm whip, rather than a jerky one. Otherwise, you'll tighten up physically and mentally.

Finally, even under severe time limitations, some weight transfer toward the target can add enough speed to the ball to make it a winner. You can generate a tremendous amount of ball speed by combining just a few of these principles.

Practice and more practice emphasizes flexibility and creativity. It's great to be able to calculate all sorts of trivial measures, such as force and momentum, but those things are only good in locker-room talk. When you have a split second to respond to a ball coming fast, you have to react naturally and feel the shot, not think it. Practice getting this "feel"—reacting comfortably to balls coming at you.

TECHNIQUE

Let's look at some factors involved in hitting the quick forehand. I've already discussed the major factors of flexible wrist action, good contact point, whipping swing and directed weight transfer. You also have to concentrate on footwork, grip, ball spin, and position recovery.

Footwork—There's not much you can do about footwork if the ball is already close to you. But the thing to remember is that you can still hit the ball hard in an open stance facing the front wall. You just have to learn how to stay calm in a nonideal position.

Hit the ball with an open stance or in whatever stance you happen to have at the time. But do it with offensive purpose, not defensively. You'll notice that even with toes pointed at the front wall, you can still turn your upper body almost parallel to the side wall. This movement winds you up like a rubber band, ready to unwind into the ball.

OPEN-STANCE SHOOTING
1) Here's the basic open stance—ready for a shot to either side.

2) In this case, a forehand is necessary. The right hip shifts back, as do the right arm and wrist.

3) Now weight starts moving toward the ball as the arm whips forward.

4) Impact and follow-through bring you back to good balance and ready for a response.

If you do have a chance to move, I recommend moving the right foot away from the approaching ball, rather than stepping into the ball with the left foot. By beginning the swing during this motion, you are ready to meet the ball as the right foot gets into place. This movement takes only a split second—just about the time you have. Of course, if you have more time, you may want to move farther from the ball to contact it from a lower position.

Grip—Although top players will tell you they use only one or two grips, they probably have five or six. One or two are used when they have time to set up for a shot. Grip is only important when you are trying to hit with maximum efficiency. When you're jammed, use what you have.

The one-grip player has an advantage because he never has to change grip. The two-grip player is wise to choose one grip—backhand, or in between—that he can use in all cases except when he has time to change grip. But in either case, don't worry much about grip.

You can adjust the direction of the shot by modifying wrist snap and sometimes the swing. Wrist snap is the most important part of making a quick forehand shot work. That's why it makes sense sometimes to practice hitting from off-balance positions using irregular grips. You want to feel comfortable making fine adjustments with the wrist.

Ball Spin—This is sometimes helpful but not as significant as in tennis. I almost never try to use extra spin purposely because it's more trouble than it's worth. A racquetball just doesn't react like a tennis ball. But if I'm jammed, and the ball gets behind me, I'll swing over the ball from behind my right hip and put it into a corner. Or, I'll try to hit it down the line.

The topspin is not for deception. Consider it protection and control. If I use a regular flat shot with the ball far behind my body, I'll either hurt my shoulder or hit the ball out of control. Adding topspin lets me swing with full force, yet control the ball.

Recovery—Finally, any shot has to be followed up. Think in terms of offense. Even if the shot was great, the other player may still return it. Think ahead. Anticipate where your opponent's return will go, and react.

Weight Transfer—Good weight transfer is another element in hitting a fast ball. Even in an awkward position, you should try to start with the weight deep in your stance. Then transfer it with your legs and hips in the direction of the intended shot.

This motion may be as little as thrusting the knees about six inches toward the front wall, to a full transfer of hip weight from rear to front foot. This motion, along with the upper body uncoiling, should be sufficient to hit the ball with good pace. One major mistake is to contact the ball too early. The result is usually a ball that sails into the left wall. That's why you should contact the ball deep in the stance. The uncoiling motion transfers that part of the motion directed at the front wall. The follow-through in this case is for balance.

Earlier I said that the contact point at times will be much deeper than you would expect. But to get maximum power, you have to move your arm and shoulder as far back as they go. Too often, the beginner will not bring his arm all the way back because he wants to be prepared for a bad bounce. This is wrong! Wrist adjustment and footwork allow you to adjust to bad bounce.

The swing must be a fluid, whipping, pendulum motion. Imagine yourself snapping a towel. For a quick forehand the motion is similar. The difference is that the arm motion has to adjust to the height of the ball.

More on Wrist Snap—Under the worst conditions, you may not have time to execute a modern windup. But you can still hit the ball with pace. The key again is to add plenty of wrist snap. If need be, you can hit with a punching, volley motion and lots of wrist snap. The half-volley is such a shot.

In hitting the half-volley, try to keep the racquet head above the wrist and your knees slightly bent to maintain control. Hit the ball either flat or with a little topspin. Start with a short backswing but lots of wrist snap. As your timing improves, you can add a full windup.

The wrist snap is last in the hitting sequence. When your motion starts for any shot, there's very little adjustment you can make—except to modify the wrist snap. You must be able to feel the plane of the racquet face. With few exceptions, snap the wrist so the racquet face comes straight through the ball, rather than over or under it.

This means that you can hit a forehand with a backhand grip. The sooner you learn to hit every shot with lots of wrist snap, the sooner your wrist will be conditioned to make the adjustments described. Wrist adjustment isn't easy at first, so you'll have to build up to it. But if you start by consciously hitting all basic shots with wrist snap, the transition to advanced or championship play will be much quicker.

PRACTICE DRILLS

Practicing the quick forehand can be dangerous because you may think that every shot should be hit with that motion. After that warning, I'll describe two drills to make your quick shots better.

In the first drill, you stand facing the front wall behind the back service line. Stand in an open stance. Tap the ball to the front wall and get the feel of the deep contact point. After a few minutes, move closer to the front wall. Do this until you get to the front service line.

Then move back and do the same thing but add more wrist and arm motion to the shot to pick up the pace. Try to "feel" the shot. The final stage is to alternate between setting yourself up and whipping a forehand down the wall. Stay in an open stance.

If you have a partner, trade off giving the other faster and faster shots. The ultimate shot from this position is the pinch.

In the second drill, alternate from side to side. Hit pinch shots from the short line. Increase the tempo as you loosen up. At first, concentrate individually on each separate point I've made. Work on wrist snap and the arm whip. When it seems easy, move closer to the front wall.

Doubles is excellent for testing what you've learned. You find yourself in close quarters with three other players.

SUMMARY

The basic principles outlined here apply to both forehand and backhand. In fact, they apply to all shots. You may not be able to follow every aspect of what I've described, but this should give you a glimpse of what is possible. As you become used to hitting quick shots, refine their execution. When they are easy, you've become an advanced player.

CHAPTER NINETEEN

Tournament Preparation

Tournament play is what you make of it. You can meet a lot of nice people, learn new shots and tactics, and get inspiration to work on your game. Tournaments can also be awful experiences if you are unprepared physically or mentally.

In this chapter I discuss tournament preparation for the serious player. Although the specific details of how I prepare may not directly apply to your needs, the general concepts will. If you want to play tournaments, but are not extremely serious about it, moderate some of the preparation accordingly.

TIMING

About six weeks before the Nationals, I begin intensive training. If I start too soon, my intensity will burn out before the end of the tournament. If I start too late, I won't reach my target of physical skills and mental preparedness. I want to peak at the Nationals, not before or after.

OVERLOADING

I spend the first three weeks overloading my physical and mental systems. It's three weeks of torture I endure because it ultimately produces the necessary mental and physical toughness.

I get up at 7 a.m. every morning and eat a medium-sized breakfast, but nothing special. Between 8 a.m. and 9 a.m., I head to a club to play for six hours—with an interruption only for lunch. I do this for six hours per day, five days per week, for three weeks! It doesn't matter whom I play. It's the on-court time that's important.

The first week is almost unbearable. After each day's workout, I eat dinner and collapse. Surprisingly, my body adapts to the workload after a week. I get accustomed to the regimen. By doubling my normal workout prior to the Nationals, I'm trying to reach the next physical plateau. My body adapts to the intensity like a weightlifter's muscle eventually adapts to increased weight.

However, one word of caution before you emulate me. This level of practice works because of early season workouts of two or three hours of play per day. I've built up a conditioning base that allows me to double my workout when necessary. You have to scale your workouts relative to your established base.

The other reason for doubling the workout is to create reserve strength. Workouts have to be longer, harder and tougher than any match will ever be. This way, if I fall behind in a match, I can still increase the tempo of play by drawing on reserve strength.

This gives me added confidence too. Not only confidence from knowing that I have reserve, but confidence that I endured three weeks of workouts tougher than any other player is willing to endure. This means I can apply more pressure than anyone else.

REMAINDER OF WORKOUT

After the first three weeks I've reached the next strength plateau, but my energy reserves are low. Tired muscles haven't had a chance to completely rebuild. During the last three weeks of the workout, I rebuild both muscles and energy reserves.

In weeks four and five, I cut back to four hours of playing per day, five days per week. In the sixth week, I cut down to two hours of playing per day. By the end of six weeks, the time I do play is more intense, but shorter. The result is greater energy and endurance.

About Carbohydrate Loading—This is a regimen of high levels of exercise for four or five days and eating below-normal amounts of carbohydrates. The intent is to deplete your body of glycogen, the fuel for quick energy.

When you then switch to a normal level of exercise, you eat more carbohydrates than usual. Your body creates more glycogen from the carbohydrates and ostensibly stores more glycogen for more energy reserves.

Carbohydrate loading is done by some athletes and ignored by others. Although I do not use carbohydrate loading, the energy buildup from my training program is similar to the desired effects.

SHOT FLEXIBILITY

The first three weeks are focused on breaking through the physical barrier. The last three weeks are aimed at breaking through the mental barrier. The attack begins by improving *shot flexibility.* This is a measure of the range of shots you can hit from a given position. The more I can hit, the greater my deception will be.

For good shot flexibility, you must be relaxed and hit with a natural, fluid swing. You have to hit shots over and over again until the timing is certain. That's why I emphasize maximum swings during practice matches—don't worry about the score.

That's also why I play long hours rather than practice alone before important tournaments. When I hit alone, I'm not under the same pressure to time shots. I don't get the same variety of shooting situations either.

Maximum shooting flexibility means that I can shoot down the wall, crosscourt, drive either direction, hit a pinch or a reverse pinch all from the same court position. Substantial wrist strength makes it possible to hit all of these shots with almost the same swing.

BE SPECIFIC

Note that so far I haven't mentioned anything but playing racquetball during my intensive training. In addition to play, I also try to run about five miles at the end of each day. I don't lift weights or run agility courses. It's too late in the season for that. If necessary, do it at the beginning of the season. Out of habit, I do some pushups and situps too.

In short, practice racquetball primarily by playing racquetball. Exclude anything not specifically related to playing racquetball. Although I do run in my late-season workouts, I do it mostly for relaxation.

FOCUS

The final weeks of preparation are aimed at honing my aggressiveness, shot-making and concentration. When cutting back on workout duration, I channel the same energy level into a shorter time period. Having stretched my shot range to its maximum in the first three or four weeks, I refine my bread-and-butter shots.

By the end of the sixth week, I have developed a finely focused aggression. At this point, I am interested only in winning each point in the quickest possible way. I now literally attack the ball with full power at every possible opportunity.

FOOD AND REST

Adequate rest is as important as all other elements of the workout. Without proper rest you cannot get maximum benefit from each training day. You won't play your best at the end of the training period.

After each day's workout, I forget about racquetball. On weekends I engage in noncompetitive activities. This is when my body can recover. Recovery time depends on your base. It may take a few seasons for you to be able to play two hours a day, three or four times per week. Successive applications of overload and rest will decrease your recovery periods.

I eat well-balanced meals. I don't drink, smoke or take drugs.

CONCLUSION

This is just a glimpse at intensive racquetball training. You can apply the general principles to training for any event:

1) Time the training period for adequate overload and recovery.

2) Use the overload method to reach the next physical plateau in minimum time.

3) Follow the overload period with a workout cutback to build up energy reserves.

4) Workout intensity should be tougher than those of real matches.

5) Work on shot flexibility and timing by playing.

6) Play to improve.

7) Get adequate rest relative to your conditioning and workout.

It would be great to use this program for every tournament. Unfortunately, nobody can. Even I can endure it just once a year. But the basic principles are useful guidelines for tailoring your individual program.

CHAPTER TWENTY

Doubles

A good singles player is not necessarily a good doubles player. In doubles, good teamwork and pinpoint accuracy are more essential than endurance and power. Coverage zones and strategies are completely different in doubles. It is usually a thinking person's game, requiring neither a full range of shots nor court coverage.

At best, doubles is entertaining to watch and play. You'll see fast forecourt exchanges, lunging backcourt gets, adrenalin-pumping drive volleys, point-stopping kills and precisely angled pinch shots. At worst, doubles is chaos.

Unless every person in a foursome understands how to play doubles, the game will be close to its worst. Four players in a small area playing a fast game can become dangerous too. This is why I recommend that beginners avoid doubles until they have basic singles skills.

Doubles can be both safe and enjoyable if you observe normal court etiquette and refrain from unsafe shots. Always give the other team room for a full, unobstructed swing. Leave the primary hitting lanes—down-the-wall, crosscourt and pinch—unobstructed.

TEAMWORK

Before stepping on the court, your team should decide on a general plan. Divide court-coverage responsibilities. If you are playing together for the first time, discuss what serves and shots you are most likely to hit under common situations. Pregame communication eliminates some of the surprises that occur during matches and improves your chances for victory.

Also decide who will be the signal-caller of the team. This person decides who takes the shot when necessary. He calls out "Yours" or "Mine" to keep play clear.

During breaks in the play, discuss what adjustments are necessary. These discussions help you regroup and focus on the best avenues of attack.

FORMATIONS

Formations are designed to divide the responsibilities for court coverage among team members. This way each player covers less than full court, reducing the potential for collisions.

There are three popular formations—side-by-side, modified side-by-side and front-and-back. You will probably use more than one formation when the situation dictates. Furthermore, the division of responsibilities does not preclude a teammate from momentarily usurping his partner's responsibilities. Do it quickly to end a rally or fill a void if your partner is out of position.

Side-by-Side—This formation is the most popular. The court is divided in half by an imaginary line running down the center from forecourt to backcourt. The player on the right is responsible for all balls coming into the right side of the court, and vice-versa.

When a left-hander teams with a right-hander, the left-hander usually covers the left side. This is an effective combination because it has forehands covering both down-the-wall scoring lanes. It is tough to score against a left/right team because the weakest zone is up the middle. The player with the stronger backhand usually takes balls moving through the middle.

When two right-handers play together, the player with the stronger backhand usually plays the left side. He covers the left wall with his backhand and takes balls through the middle with his forehand. For two left-handers on the same team, the above logic applies in reverse.

Modified Side-by-Side—Usually, this formation is used by a team of right-handers. The court is divided diagonally by an imaginary line running from the left-front corner to the right-rear corner.

The player on the left plays a little deeper than he would in the side-by-side formation. The player on the right plays a little shallower. Coverage zones are about the same as in side-by-side but are rotated slightly counterclockwise.

The formation is surprisingly effective because it allows the left-side player to protect his backhand, even against a left-hander's forehand. Also, because of the skewed coverage zones, the backhand scoring lane opens up a little more.

Front-and-Back—This is also called the *I formation*. It is usually used by a team with a quick forecourt shooter and a powerful backcourt shooter/retriever. The court is divided laterally by an imaginary line at midcourt that parallels the short line. The front player roams the middle of the service zone. The back player floats in backcourt. The front player must cover all pinch shots and soft kills. The back player must cover all other shots.

This formation was much more popular in the early days of racquetball. You may still find it at local clubs when a stronger player teams with a weaker one. The weaker player can stay up front where his limited talents will not get in the way during long ceiling rallies and drives. He becomes effective when the ball sets up in the forecourt. Even so, this formation does not provide enough of an offensive advantage to be useful in advanced play.

However, the front-back formation does arise during rallies that drive a player to a rear corner. This can force his partner to cover the forecourt until the first player gets back into position. The team returns to normal formation when the backcourt player recovers.

CENTERCOURT CONTROL

Holding centercourt is even more important in doubles than singles. If your team can maintain centercourt position while keeping the other team in back court, you will have several advantages:

1) You will have better angles for scoring.

2) You will partially block the view of the ball, leaving the other team with less time to react.

3) You will be more accurate because you are close to the front wall.

If you are skilled enough to keep your opposition in backcourt, use the side-by-side formation, even if you are a modified side-by-side team. Unfortunately, front-and-back-formation teams usually find it difficult to assume a side-by-side formation.

A common mistake in the side-by-side or modified formation is to stand too close to the side walls. Both players should stay away from the side walls because you can get trapped there when the ball starts zooming around the court. It's better to stand almost next to each other so you don't get jammed or pinned against a wall. You won't collide if each member knows his responsibilities. Defer to your partner when he enters your territory.

SERVING

Service strategy in doubles is basically the same as in singles. The one exception concerns your partner's position. Avoid serves that keep your partner from entering the play. In addition, you can use some serves in doubles that would normally be unwise in singles.

The most popular are Z and lob serves. In doubles, you want the opposition to shoot the ball while your team is physically in front of them. If they miss, your team will have an easy shot with the opposition trapped in back.

The Z serve is low enough to be tempting, but high enough to prevent a rollout. Both the Z and lob serves give your partner enough time to move out of the service box, where he must stand until the ball crosses the short line. The low Z serve through centercourt is an effective serve against a left/right team because you hit it to two backhands facing the middle.

Avoid drive and half-lob serves that pin your partner to the side wall. If

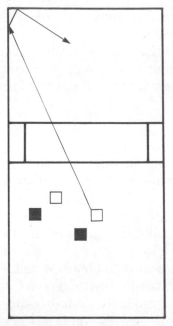

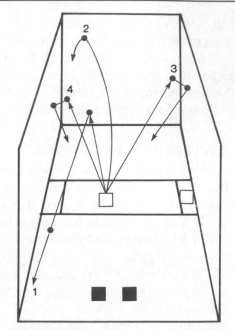

Hit a pinch when your opponents are behind you or when you are partially blocking the appropriate coverage zone.

These are good serves to use in doubles: (1) drive, (2) lob, (3) forehand Z and (4) backhand Z.

your partner is on the left, and you serve a drive serve to the left-rear corner, he won't move out of the service box to assume his defensive position. Either he will be out of position and not help you cover the court, or he will get hit by the ball. You need his help, so avoid these serves. There are plenty of others to use.

Service Return—In most cases, you should return the serve with a ceiling shot. In singles, you had to contend with just one player. In doubles, you have two people waiting for a setup. If you are lucky enough to drive the return past one player, the other player can still kill the ball.

Shoot or drive weak serves against a player who doesn't move out of the service box, or against a team that doesn't have good kill shots. If your partner moves quickly to centercourt while you are returning serve, he can cover an attempted kill of your return.

Be careful with crosscourt drives. Unless perfect, they will be cut off by the other team. This will leave you and your partner out of position. However, a crosscourt drive is particularly effective if hit at a player who tends to stay in the service box after his partner serves. The ball will be coming at his knees, leaving him little time to react.

CEILING SHOT

Often a rally begins as a ceiling rally because of the difficulty of gaining an offensive advantage on a service return. When this happens, hit ceiling shots to the left-side player's backhand. This means centercourt for a left/right team and the left side for a right/right team. Have patience and stick with the ceiling rally until you get a setup or a chance to drive an overhead at a weak opponent.

Typically, one player relaxes after a few successive ceiling shots and either drifts toward a side wall or stands still. An overhead drive can then win a point or force a weak return.

VOLLEY

The volley is an important shot in doubles because it allows you to maintain centercourt position. Also, a quick punch into a corner can end a rally when an opponent is waiting for a hard drive volley.

PINCH SHOT

The pinch shot is particularly useful when the opposition is on the

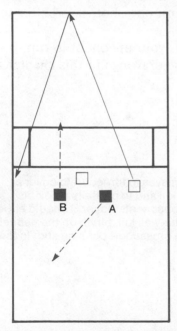

Drive the ball crosscourt when player B anticipates the pinch and starts moving toward forecourt. Player A may cover the shot, but that leaves the right side open for your next shot.

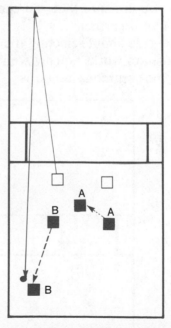

Player A moves to centercourt to cover the forecourt for his partner. Player B should either hit a ceiling shot or drive the ball down the left wall. Player B should not make a crosscourt shot because it would put his partner out of position.

defensive. When they start leaning back instead of challenging you in centercourt, hit the pinch.

Also use it to scramble the opposition's formation, testing their ability to regain proper court positions. Mix your pinch shots with down-the-wall kills and wide-angled crosscourts. But use the latter only if it is clear that your partner won't be caught out of position and your opponent has not moved up to cover your pinch.

SHOT SELECTION

Doubles has a peculiar strategy called *isolation strategy.* In this case, almost all balls are directed at one player. The intent in the short run is to attack the weaker player and keep the better player cold. When a ball is finally hit to the better player, he will be cold because he hasn't had many chances to touch the ball.

If during a rally, your partner gets way out of position, such as falling on the floor, hit a ceiling shot to allow him enough time to recover. If you go for a kill and miss, or if you go for a pass, your opponents will exploit your partner. Unless you are sure that you can end the rally on one shot, it is better to buy time for your partner.

The rule about selecting the shot that forces your opponent to run through your position works equally well in doubles. The drawings in this chapter illustrate some common situations.

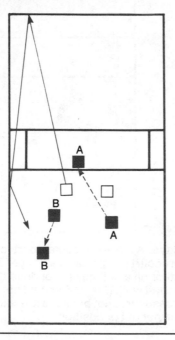

Player A moves to forecourt to cover a potential kill and to partially block his left-side opponent. Player B should either try a down-the-wall kill, pinch on the near side or make a crosscourt passing shot to the right.

Glossary

Ace—A legal first serve that the receiver does not return.

Alley shot—See *down-the-wall shot*.

Anticipation—Predicting and covering shots by reading an opponent's intentions from his body language.

Around-the-wall ball—A defensive shot that first hits high on the side wall, the front wall, then the other side wall before finally striking the floor between centercourt and backcourt.

Avoidable hinder—Any intentional hinder or an unintentional hinder of an obvious scoring shot. The offender either loses the serve or a point.

Backcourt—Court area behind the short line.

Back wall—Rear wall.

Back-wall shot—A shot made after the ball rebounds off the back wall.

Block—A maneuver done to prevent an opponent from viewing or getting to the ball. It is a hinder.

Bottom board—The bottom one inch of the front wall. "Going for the bottom board" means trying to make a rollout.

Butt—Enlarged end of the racquet handle.

Ceiling ball—A defensive shot that strikes the ceiling first, the front wall and then the floor. It rebounds deep into backcourt.

Centercourt—The court area that extends from the short line to about 10 feet behind the short line.

Centercourt control—Maintaining position in centercourt.

Change-up—A shot hit softer than normal to disrupt your opponent's timing.

Choke—Psyched out.

Choke up—To grip the racquet closer to the racquet head than usual.

Closed face—The top of the racquet face tilted forward.

Closed stance—Feet placement causing the body to turn partially away from the front wall.

Club play—Informal competition.

Cocked wrist position—Ready position of wrist in shot-making.

Control—The ability to consistently place the ball in an intended spot.

Corner shot—See *pinch shot*.

Court hinder—An unavoidable hinder due to the interference of a rally by a court obstacle, such as a door latch.

Coverage zone—Court area where a player must be to return an opponent's shot.

Crosscourt drive—A sharply hit shot striking the front wall and crossing over to the other side of the court.

Crotch ball—A shot striking where two playing surfaces join, such as the front wall/floor juncture.

Crowding—Playing too close to an opponent.

Cutthroat—A racquetball game with three players. Each player during his serve plays against and scores points against the other two. Serve rotates among players when the server loses serve.

Defensive shot—A shot intended to prolong a rally rather than end it.

Doughnut—Scoring zero points in a game.

Doubles—A game played between two two-player teams.

Down-the-wall shot—A shot striking the front wall and running along a side wall. Also called a *down-the-line* or *alley shot.*

Drive serve—A low, sharply hit serve that does not strike a side wall until passing the short line.

Drop shot—A soft kill shot, also called a *dump shot.*

Fault—An illegal serve.

Five-foot line—Receiving line.

Flail—Slang term for swinging with maximum speed.

Fly shot—A volley.

Foot fault—Illegal placement of a foot during a serve.

Freak ball—A shot taking an unexpected bounce.

Forecourt—Court area in front of the short line.

Garbage serve—Half-lob serve.

Half-lob serve—A 10-foot high lob serve.

Half-volley—To strike the ball immediately after it bounces on the floor. To short hop the ball.

High-lob serve—A 15-foot high lob serve.

I formation—Doubles formation in which one player is responsible for covering the forecourt. The other player is responsible for covering the backcourt.

Isolation strategy—Doubles strategy of hitting almost all shots to one player and very few to his partner.

Junk serve—Half-lob serve.

Kill shot—Shot that hits so low on the front wall that a return is impossible.

Lob serve—A soft serve hit 10 to 15 feet into the air.

Long serve—Any serve that carries to the back wall before striking the floor.

Near-side pinch—Pinch shot hit into the side wall, in front of the player.

Offensive shot—An aggressive shot intended to end the rally.

One-grip system—Using one grip for both forehand and backhand shots.

Open face—Top of the racquet face tilted backward.

Open stance—Foot placement causing the body to partially face the front wall.

Passing shot—Shot going past an opponent.

Pendulum swing—Arm motion resembling the motion of a pendulum.

Pinch shot—Kill shot hit into a front corner, side wall first.

Plum—An easy setup shot.

Power zone—Area between your waist and your knees where a ball can be hit with maximum power.

Rally—Exchange of shots during play.

Ready position—Semicrouched body position assumed when waiting for the next shot.

Receiving line—The line behind which a service receiver must stand. A receiver cannot strike a service return until the serve has crossed this line or bounced on the floor.

Reverse pinch—Pinch shot hit into the side wall, behind the player.

Rollout—Kill shot that strikes so low on the front wall that it rolls out unplayable.

Scoring zone—Court area where you score a high percentage of points.

Screen ball—A visual hinder where the ball comes so close to a player's body that it can't be seen by the other player.

Service box—An area on both sides of the service zone where a doubles player must stand when his teammate is serving.

Service line—Front line, parallel to and five feet in front of the short line.

Shooter—Aggressive player whose game strategy revolves around attempting to kill almost all setups.

Shoot the ball—To hit a kill shot.

Short line—Line halfway between and parallel to the front and back walls past which a serve must carry before hitting the floor.

Short serve—Serve that fails to carry beyond the short line.

Side-by-side—Doubles formation in which each player is responsible for covering his side of the court.

Sideout—Loss of service with the server and receiver exchanging positions.

Side-wall/front-wall kill—Pinch shot.

Singles—A racquetball game in which two players compete against each other.

Skip ball—Ball that hits the floor before reaching the front wall.

Splat—Wide pinch shot hit with high velocity from backcourt near a side wall.

Straddle ball—Ball that passes through the legs of a player after rebounding from the front wall.

Straight-in kill—Kill shot that parallels a side wall.

Three-wall serve—Illegal serve that strikes three walls on the fly.

Topspin—Ball rotation due to the racquet head coming over the top of the ball.

Touch shot—A shot that is "placed," not powered.

Tournament play—Formal competition.

Tour of the court—Drawn-out rally in which one player exerts little effort while running his opponent all over the court.

Trigger-finger grip—Method of holding the racquet as if it were a pistol.

Two-grip system—Using different grips for the backhand and the forehand.

Unavoidable hinder—Interference of normal play brought about unintentionally by a player, the court, equipment or other hindrance.

Underspin—Ball rotation due to the racquet head coming under the ball.

V ball—Crosscourt shot.

Volley—Hitting the ball before it bounces.

Wallpaper ball—Shot that hugs a side wall so closely that it is difficult to return.

Winner—Offensive shot that wins a rally.

Z ball—Shot that hits high on the front wall, ricochets quickly into the near side wall, then travels to the opposite side wall before striking the floor.

Z serve—Serve resembling the Z ball, but strikes the floor after striking the first side wall.

AARA Rules

I THE GAME

A. Types of Games—Racquetball may be played by two, three or four players. When played by two it is called *singles;* when played by three, *cutthroat;* and when played by four, *doubles.*

B. Description—Racquetball, as the name implies, is a competitive game in which only one racquet is used by each player to serve and return the ball.

C. The Objective—The objective is to win each rally by serving or returning the ball so the opponent is unable to keep the ball in play. A rally is over when a side makes an error, is unable to return the ball before it touches the floor twice, or if a hinder is called.

D. Points and Outs—Points are scored only by the server, or serving team, when it serves an ace or wins a rally. When the serving side loses a rally, it loses the serve. Losing the serve is called an *out* in singles, and a *handout* or *sideout* in doubles.

E. Game—A game is won by the side first scoring 15 points. The third game, referred to as the *tiebreaker,* is played to 11. It is necessary to win a game by only one point.

F. Match—A match is won by the first side winning two games. The first two games of a match are played to 15 points. In the event each side wins one game, the match shall be decided by an 11-point tiebreaker.

G. Doubles Team—A doubles team consists of two players that meet either the age requirements or player-classification requirements to participate in a particular division of play. A team must be classified by the ability level, or player classification, of the higher ranked player on the team.

A change in playing partners may not be made after the final draw has been made and posted. Under no circumstances can a partner change be made during the course of a tournament without the consent of the Tournament Director.

H. Consolation Matches—The following considerations apply:

1) Consolation matches may be waived at the discretion of the Tournament Director, but this waiver must be in writing on the tournament application.

2) In all AARA-sanctioned tournaments each entrant shall be entitled to participate in a minimum of two matches. This then means that losers of their first match have the opportunity to compete in a consolation bracket of their own division. In draws of less than seven players, a round-robin format may be offered.

3) Preliminary matches will be two of three games to 11 points. Semifinals and finals matches will follow the regular scoring format.

II COURTS AND EQUIPMENT

A. Courts—Specifications for the standard four-wall racquetball court follow:

1) Dimensions: The dimensions shall be 20 feet wide, 20 feet high, and 40 feet long, with a back wall at least 12 feet high. All surfaces within the court shall be deemed ''in play'' with the exception of any gallery openings or surfaces designated as *court hinders.*

2) Lines And Zones: Racquetball courts shall be divided and marked with 1-1/2 inch wide lines as follows:

a) *Short Line*—The back edge of the short line is midway between (20 feet) and parallel to the front and back walls, thus dividing the court into equal front and back courts.

b) *Service Line*—The front edge of the service line is parallel with and located five feet in front of the back edge of the short line.

c) *Service Zone*—The service zone is the area between the outer edges of the short and service lines.

d) *Service Boxes*—The service boxes are located at each end of the service zone and designated by lines parallel with each side wall. The inside edge of the lines are 18 inches from the side walls.

e) *Receiving Line*—Five feet back of the short line, vertical lines shall be marked on each side wall extending three to six inches from the floor. The back edge of the receiving lines shall be five feet from the back edge of the short line.

IMPORTANT NOTE—The following receiving line is recommended for adoption, effective September 1, 1986: A non-solid line five feet back of the short line. The receiving line is designated on the court floor by 21-inch lines parallel to the front wall that extend from each side wall and are connected by a series of six-inch lines separated by six-inch spaces (16 six-inch lines and 17 six-inch spaces). The back edge of the receiving lines shall be five feet from the back edge of the short line.

f) *Safety Zone*—This is the five-foot area bounded by the short line and the receiving line. The zone is observed only during the serve. Entering the zone prematurely if the receiver commits the infraction, results in a point for the server. Entering the zone prematurely if the server commits the infraction, results in loss of serve. (See Rules 8A and 7I.)

B. Ball Specifications—These are as follows:

1) The standard racquetball shall be 2-1/4-inch in diameter; weigh approximately 1.4 ounces, and at a temperature of 70F to 74F, with a 100-inch drop rebound between 68 and 72 inches; hardness at 55 to 60 inches measured by a durometer.

2) Any ball that carries the endorsement of approval form the AARA is an official ball. Only AARA-approved balls may be used in AARA-sanctioned tournaments.

C. Ball Selection—The following considerations apply:

1) A ball shall be selected by the referee for use in each match. During the match, the referee either at his discretion, or at the request of a player or team, may replace the game balls. Balls that are not round or that bounce erratically will not be used.

2) In tournament play, the referee and the players will agree to an alternate ball, so that in the event of breakage, the second ball can be put into play immediately.

D. Racquet Specifications—Regulation specifications are as follows:

1) Dimensions: The total length and width of the racquet may not exceed 27 inches. The length of the racquet may not exceed 20-1/2 inches and the head width may not exceed 9 inches. These measurements are computed from the outer edge of the rims, not including bumper guard, and from the farthest solid part of the handle.

2) A regulation racquet frame may be of any material, as long as it conforms to the above specifications.

3) A regulation racquet frame must include a thong that must be securely attached to the player's wrist.

4) Racquet string should be gut, monofilament, nylon, graphite, plastic, metal, or a combination thereof, providing strings do not mark or deface the ball.

E. Uniform—Regulation uniforms have the following characteristics:

1) The uniform and shoes may be of any color, but the shoes must have soles that do not mark or damage the court floor. The shirt may contain any insignia or writing considered in good taste by the Tournament Director. Players are required to wear shirts. Extremely loose fitting or otherwise distracting garments are not permitted.

2) Eye protection is required for any participant under the age of 19 in all AARA sanctioned tournaments.

III OFFICIATING AND PLAY REGULATIONS

Rule 1A: Tournaments—All tournaments shall be managed by a committee or Tournament Director who shall designate the officials.

Rule 1B: Officials—The official shall be a referee designated by the Tournament Director, floor manager or one agreed to by both participants or teams in doubles. Officials may also include, at the discretion of the Tournament Director, a scorekeeper and two linespeople.

Rule 1C: Removal of Referee—A referee may be removed upon the agreement of both participants, teams in doubles or at the discretion of the Tournament Director or rules officials. In the event that a referee's removal is requested by one player or team and not agreed to by the other, the Tournament Director or officials may accept or reject the request.

Rule 1D: Rule Briefing—Before all tournaments, all officials and players shall be briefed on rules and on court hinders or regulations or modification the Tournament Director wishes to impose. The briefing should be in writing. Current AARA rules will apply and be made available. Any modifications the Tournament Director wishes to impose must be stated on the entry form and in writing and be available to all players at registration time.

Rule 1E: Referees—The many responsibilities of the referees follow:

1) Pre-match: Before each match begins, it is the duty of the referee to:

   a) Check the adequacy of court preparation with respect to cleanliness, lighting and temperature.

   b) Check the availability and suitability of materials—including balls, towels, scorecards, pencils and timepiece—necessary for the match.

   c) Go on court to instruct players.

   d) Point out court hinders and note any local regulations.

   e) Inspect equipment and toss coin.

   f) Check linespeople and scorekeeper and ask for reserve game ball upon assuming officiating position.

   g) Review any rule modification in effect for a particular tournament.

2) Decisions: During the match, the referee shall make all decisions with regard to the rules. Where linespeople are used, the referee shall announce all final judgments. If both players in singles and three out of four in a doubles match disagree with a judgment call made by the referee, the referee is overruled. The referee shall have jurisdiction over the spectators as well as players while the match is in progress.

3) Protests: Any decision not involving the judgment of the referee may, on protest, be decided by the Tournament Director or designated official.

4) Forfeitures: A match may be forfeited by the referee when

   a) Any player or team refuses to abide by the referee's decision, or engages in unsportsmanlike conduct;

   b) A player or team fails to comply with the tournament or host facility's rules while on the premises, for failure to referee, for improper conduct on the premises between matches, or for abuse of hospitality, locker room or other rules and procedures;

c) Any player or team fails to report to play 10 minutes after the match has been scheduled to play. (The Tournament Director may permit a longer delay if circumstances warrant such a decision.)

5) Other Rulings: The referee may rule on all matters not covered in the AARA Official Rules. However, the referee may be overruled by the Tournament Director.

Rule 1F.1: Linespeople—Two linespeople are recommended for all matches from the semifinals on up, subject to availability and subject to the discretion of the tournament officials. The linespeople shall be selected by the officials and situated as designated by the officials. If any player objects to the selection of a linesperson before the match begins, all reasonable effort will be made to find a replacement acceptable to the officials and players. If a player or team objects to a linesperson after the match begins, replacement will be under the discretion of the referee and officials.

Rule 1F.2: Linespeople—Linespeople are designated to help decide appealed rulings. Two linespeople will be designated by the referee and will, at the referee's signal, either agree or disagree with the referee's ruling. The signal by a linesperson to show agreement with the referee is *thumbs up*. The signal to show disagreement is *thumbs down*. The signal for no opinion is *open-palm down*.

If both linespeople signal no opinion, the referee's call stands. If both linespeople disagree with the referee, the referee must reverse the ruling. If one linesperson agrees and one disagrees or has no opinion, the referee's call stands. If one linesperson disagrees and one has no opinion, rally or serve shall be replayed. Any replays will result in two serves with the exception of appeals on the second serve itself.

Rule 1G: Appeals—In any match using line judges, a player or team may appeal only the following calls or non-calls by the referee—kill shots and skip balls; fault serves; out serves; double-bounce pickups; receiving the violations; rule interpretations.

The appeal must be directed to the referee, who then will request opinions simultaneously from the two linepersons. Any appeal made directly to the linepersons by a player or team or made after an excessive demonstration or complaint by the player(s) will be considered void and any appeal rights for that side for that particular rally will be forfeited.

1) Kill Shot Appeals: If the referee makes a call of "good" on a kill shot attempt that ends a particular rally, the loser of the rally may appeal the call. If the appeal is successful and the referee's original call reversed, the side that originally lost the rally is declared the winner of the rally. If the referee makes the call of "bad" or "skip" on a kill shot attempt, the rally has ended and the side against whom the call was made has the right to appeal the call if it thinks the shot good. If the appeal is successful and the referee's original call reversed, the referee must then decide if the shot could have been returned had play continued. If the shot could have been or was returned, the rally will be played. If the shot was a kill or pass that the opponent could not have retrieved (in the referee's opinion), the side that originally lost the rally is declared the winner of the rally. The referee's judgment in this matter is final. Any rally replayed will afford the server two serves.

2) Fault Serve Appeals: If the referee makes a call of "fault" on a serve, the server may appeal the call. If the appeal is successful, the server is entitled to replay the serve. If the served ball was considered by the referee to be an ace, then a point will be awarded to the server. If the referee makes "no call" on a serve (therefore indicating that the serve was "good"), either side may appeal, then the situation reverts to the point of service with the call becoming fault. If it was a first service, one more serve is allowed. If the serve was a second serve, then the fault serve would cause an out.

3) Out Serve Appeals: If the referee makes a call of "out serve" thereby stopping play, the serving side may appeal the call. If the appeal is successful, the referee shall revise the call to the

proper call and the service shall be replayed, or a point awarded if the resulting serve was an ace. If the referee makes "no call," or calls a fault serve, and the receiver feels it was an out serve, the receiver may appeal. If the appeal is successful, the serve results in an out. Note: A safety-zone violation by the server is an out serve.

4) Double-Bounce Pickup Appeals: If the referee makes a call of "two bounces," thereby stopping play, the side against whom the call was made has the right of appeal. If the appeal is upheld, the rally is replayed or the referee may award the rally to the hitter if the resulting shot could not have been retrieved by the opponent—and providing the referee's call did not cause the opponent to hesitate or stop play. If the referee makes "no call" on a particular play, indicating that the player hit the ball before the second bounce, the opponent has a right to appeal at the end of the rally. However, since the ball is in play, the side wishing to appeal must clearly motion to the referee and linespeople by raising their non-racquet hand, thereby alerting the officials as to the exact shot that is being appealed. At the same time, the player appealing must continue to play. If the appealing player should lose the rally, and the appeal is upheld, the player who appealed then becomes the winner of the rally. All rallies replayed as the result of a double-bounce pickup appeal shall result in the server getting two serves.

5) Receiving-Line (Encroachment) Violation Appeals: If the referee makes a call of encroachment, thereby stopping play, the receiving side may appeal the call. If the appeal is successful, the service shall be replayed. If the referee makes no call and the server feels there was encroachment, the server may appeal. If the appeal is successful, the service results in a point. (For safety-zone violation by server or doubles partner, see 1G.3).

6) Rules Interpretations: If a player feels that the referee has interpreted the rules incorrectly, the player may require the referee or Tournament Director to show him the applicable rule in the rule book.

Rule 2A: Service Order—The player or side winning the toss becomes the first server and starts the first game. The loser of the toss will serve first in the second game. The player or team scoring the most total points in games one and two will serve first in the tiebreaker. In the event that both players or teams score an equal number of points in the first two games, another coin toss will determine the server in the tiebreaker.

Rule 2B: Service Start—The serve is started from any place within the service zone. No part of either foot may extend beyond either line of the service zone. Stepping on, but not over the line is permitted. The server must remain in the service zone from the moment the service motion begins until the served ball passes the short line. Violations are called *foot faults*. The server may not start any service motion until the referee has called the score or the second serve.

Rule 2C: Service Manner—Once the service motion begins, the ball is dropped or thrown to the floor while the server stands within the confines of the service zone. On the first bounce the ball is struck by the racquet so that the ball hits the front wall first. On rebound it hits the floor behind the back edge of the short line, either with or without touching one of the side walls. A *balk serve* or *fake swing* at the ball shall be deemed an infraction and be judged an out serve.

Rule 2D: Service Readiness—Serves will not be made until the receiving side is ready and the referee has called the score. The referee will call the score as both server and receiver prepare to return to their respective positions, shortly after the previous point has ended.

Rule 2E: Service Delays—Delays on the part of the server or receiver exceeding 10 seconds will result in an out or point against the offender.

1) 10-Second Rule: The rule is applicable to the server and receiver simultaneously. Collectively, they are allowed up to 10 seconds, after the score is called, to serve or be ready to receive. It is the server's responsibility to look and be certain the receiver is ready. If the receiver is not ready, he must signal so by raising his racquet above his head or completely turning his back

to the server. (These are the only two acceptable signals.)

2) If the server serves the ball while the receiver is signaling "not ready," the serve will go over with no penalty and the server will be warned by the referee to check the receiver. If the server continues to serve without checking the receiver, the referee may award a technical for delay of game.

3) After the score is called, if the server looks at the receiver and the receiver is not signaling "not ready," the server may then serve. If the receiver attempts to signal "not ready" after that point, such signal shall not be acknowledged and the serve becomes legal.

Rule 3A. Doubles Server—At the beginning of each game in doubles, each side will inform the referee of the order of service that will be followed throughout the game. When the first server is out the first time up, the side is out. Thereafter both players on each side will serve until each receives a handout.

Rule 3B: Partner's Position—On each serve, the server's partner will stand erect with back to the side wall and with both feet on the floor within the service box from the moment the server begins his service motion until the served ball passes the short line. Violations of this rule are called *foot faults*.

Rule 4: Defective Serves—There are three main types, all resulting in penalties as follows:

Rule 4A: Dead-Ball Serve—A dead-ball serve results in no penalty and the server is given another serve, without canceling a prior illegal serve.

Rule 4B: Fault Serve—Two fault serves result in a handout.

Rule 4C: Out Serve—An out serve results in a handout.

Rule 5. Dead-Ball Serves—These do not cancel any previous illegal serve. They occur when an otherwise legal serve does the following:

Rule 5A: Hits Partner—Hits the server's partner on the fly on the rebound from the front wall while the server's partner is in the service box. Any serve that touches the floor before hitting the partner in the box is short.

Rule 5B: Screen Balls—Passes so close to the server or server's partner as to obstruct the view of the returning side. Any serve passing behind the server's partner and the side wall is an automatic screen.

Rule 5C: Court Hinders—Hits any part of the court that under local rules is a dead ball.

Rule 5D: Broken Ball—If the ball is determined to have broken on the serve, a new ball will be substituted and the serve will be replayed, not canceling any prior fault serve.

Rule 6: Fault Serves—The following serves are faults and any two in succession result in an out:

Rule 6A: Foot Faults—A foot fault results when

1) The server does not begin the service motion with both feet in the service zone;

2) The server steps over the front service line before the served ball passes the short line;

3) In doubles, the server's partner is not in the service box with both feet on the floor and back to the wall from the time the server begins the service motion until the ball passes the short line. If the server, or doubles partner, enters into the safety zone before the served ball passes the short line, it will result in the loss of serve.

Rule 6B: Short Serve—A short serve is any served ball that first hits the front wall and on the rebound hits the floor on or in front of the short line with or without touching a side wall.

Rule 6C: Three-Wall Serve—Any served ball that first hits the front wall and on the rebound hits the two side walls on the fly.

Rule 6D: Ceiling Serve—Any served ball that first hits the front wall and then touches the ceiling, with or without touching a side wall.

Rule 6E: Long Serve—Any served ball that first hits the front wall and rebounds to the back wall before touching the floor, with or without touching a side wall.

Rule 6F: Out-of-Court Serve—Any served ball that first hits the front wall and, before striking the floor, goes out of the court.

Rule 7: Out Serves—Any of the following serves results in an out:

Rule 7A: Failure of Server—Failure of server to put the ball into play within 10 seconds of the calling of the score by the referee.

Rule 7B: Missed Ball—Any attempt to strike the ball that results in a total miss or in touching any part of the server's body.

Rule 7C: Non-Front Serve—Any served ball that does not strike the front wall first.

Rule 7D: Touched Serve—Any served ball that on the rebound from the front wall touches the server, or server's racquet, or any ball intentionally stopped or caught by the server or server's partner.

Rule 7E: Crotch Serve—If the served ball hits the crotch of the front wall and floor, front wall and side wall, or front wall and ceiling, it is considered "no good" and is an out serve. A serve into the crotch of the back wall and the floor is good and in play. A served ball hitting the crotch of the side wall and floor (as in a Z serve) beyond the short line is "good" and in play.

Rule 7F: Illegal Hit—Any illegal hit (contacting the ball twice, carries, or hitting the ball with the handle of the racquet or part of the body or uniform) results in an out serve.

Rule 7G: Fake or Balk Serve—Such a serve is defined as a non-continuous movement of the racquet towards the ball as the server drops the ball for the purpose of serving and results in an out serve.

Rule 7H: Out-of-Order Serve—In doubles, if it is discovered that the second server served first and is still serving, the penalty will be that the first server loses his serve. The second server may finish the inning and all points scored will count. If while the first server is serving, it is discovered that the second server served first, the penalty will be an immediate side out. All points served will count. If it is discovered that the first server served, the second server served, and the first server is serving again, the penalty will be assessment of a technical and all points scored during the first server's extra inning will be subtracted from their team.

Rule 7I: Safety-Zone Violation—If the server, or doubles partner enters into the safety zone before the served ball passes the short line, it will result in the loss of serve.

Rule 8: Return of Serve—The following rules cover service return:

Rule 8A: Receiving Position—The receiver may not
1) Enter the safety zone until the ball bounces.
2) Strike the ball until the ball breaks the plane of the receiving (5-foot) line on a fly-return attempt. The follow-through may carry the receiver or his racquet past the receiving line.
3) Break the plane of the short line with his body or racquet during the service return. Any violation by the receiver results in a point for the server.

Rule 8B: Defective Serve—The receiving side will not catch or touch a defectively served ball until a call by the referee has been made or it has touched the floor for the second time.

Rule 8C: Legal Return—After the ball is legally served, one of the players on the receiving side must strike the ball with the racquet either on the fly or after the first bounce and before the ball touches the floor the second time to return the ball to the front wall, either directly or after touching one or both side walls, the back wall or the ceiling, or any combination of those surfaces. A returned ball may not touch the floor before touching the front wall.

Rule 8D: Failure to Return—Failure to return a serve results in a point for the server.

Rule 9: Changes of Serve—Serve changes under the following conditions:

Rule 9A: Outs—A server is entitled to continue serving until:
1) Out Serve: The player commits an out serve as per rule 7.
2) Player commits two fault serves in succession as per rule 6.

3) Hits Partner: Player hits his partner with an attempted return.

4) Return Failure: Player or partner fails to hit the ball on one bounce or fails to return the ball to the front wall on a fly, with or without hitting any combination of walls and ceiling.

5) Avoidable Hinder: Player or partner commits an avoidable hinder as per rule 12.

Rule 9B: Sideout—In singles, a single handout or out, is the same as a sideout and retires the server. In doubles, a single handout is the same as a sideout on the first service of each game. Thereafter, two handouts are the same as a sideout and thereby retires the serving team.

Rule 9C: Effect—When the server, or the serving team, receives a sideout, the server(s) become(s) the receiver(s) and the receiver(s) become(s) the server(s).

Rule 10: Rallies—Each legal return after the serve is called a *rally*. Play during rallies will be according to the following rules:

Rule 10A: Legal Hits—Only the head of the racquet may be used at any time to return the ball. The racquet may be held in one or both hands. Switching hands to hit a ball, touching the ball with any part of the body or uniform, or removing the wrist thong result in loss of the rally.

Rule 10B: One Touch—In attempting returns, the ball may be touched or struck only once by a player or team. Otherwise, the result is a loss of rally. The ball may not be *carried,* which is staying on the racquet in such a way that the effect is more of a sling or throw than a hit.

Rule 10C: Failure to Return—This is defined as:

1) The ball bouncing on the floor more than once before being hit.

2) The ball not reaching the front wall on the fly.

3) The ball caroming off a player's racquet into a gallery or wall opening without first hitting the front wall.

4) A ball that obviously does not have the velocity or direction to hit the front wall that strikes another player on the court.

5) A ball struck by one player on a team hits that player's partner, or a player is struck by a ball that was previously hit by that player, or partner.

6) An avoidable hinder as per rule 12 is committed.

Rule 10D: Effect—Violations of Rules 10A, 10B and 10C result in a loss of rally. If the serving player or team loses the rally, it is a handout or sideout. If the receiver(s) loses the rally, it results in a point for the server(s).

Rule 10E: Return Attempts—The following considerations apply:

1) In singles, if a player swings at, but misses the ball, the player may continue to attempt to return the ball until it touches the floor for the second time.

2) In doubles, if one player swings at, but misses the ball, both partners may make further attempts to return the ball until it touches the floor the second time. Both partners on a side are entitled to return the ball.

Rule 10F: Out-of-Court Ball—This is defined as:

1) After Return: Any ball returned to the front wall which on the rebound or the first bounce goes into the gallery or through any opening in a sidewall. The ball will be declared dead and the server will receive two serves.

2) No Return: Any ball not returned to the front wall, but which caroms off a player's racquet into the gallery or into any opening in a sidewall either with or without touching the ceiling, side or back wall. The ball will be an out or point against the player(s) failing to make the return.

Rule 10H: Broken Ball—If there is any suspicion that a ball has broken on the serve, or during a rally, play will continue until the end of the rally. The referee or any player may request the ball be examined. If the referee decides the ball is broken, a new ball will be put into play and the server given two serves. The only proper way to check for a broken ball is to squeeze it by hand. Checking the ball by striking it with a racquet will not be considered a valid check and will work to the disadvantage of the player or team that struck the ball after the rally.

Rule 10I: Play Stoppage—If a player loses a shoe or other equipment, or foreign objects enter the court, or any outside interference occurs, the referee will stop the play if such occurrence interferes with ensuing play or player's safety.

Rule 10J: Replays—Any rallies that are replayed for any reason without the awarding of a point or sideout will result in any previous faults being canceled and the server awarded two serves.

Rule 11: Dead-Ball Hinders—These result in the rally being replayed without penalty and the server receiving two serves.

Rule 11A: Situations—Typical dead-ball hinders are as follows:

1) Court Hinders: A ball that hits any part of the court that has been designated is a court hinder, or any ball that takes an irregular bounce off a rough or irregular surface in such a manner as the referee determines that said irregular bounce affected the rally.

2) Hitting Opponent: Any returned ball that touches an opponent on the fly before it returns to the front wall. The player that has been hit or "nicked" by the ball may make this call, but it must be made immediately and acknowledged by the referee. Any ball hitting an opponent that obviously did not have the velocity or direction to reach the front wall will not result in a hinder, and will cause the player or team that hit the ball to lose the rally.

3) Body Contact: If body contact occurs that the referee believes was sufficient to stop the rally, either for the purpose of preventing injury by further contact or because the contact prevented a player from being able to make a reasonable return, the referee will award a hinder. Body contact, particularly on the follow-through, is not necessarily a hinder.

4) Screen Ball: This is any ball rebounding from the front wall close to the body of a player on the team that just returned the ball interfering with or preventing the returning player or team from seeing the ball.

5) Backswing Hinder: Any body contact either on the backswing or enroute to or just prior to returning the ball that impairs the hitter's ability to take a reasonable swing. This call may be made by the player attempting to return if it is made immediately and is subject to acceptance and approval of the referee. Note: The interference may be construed as an avoidable hinder. (See Rule 12E.)

6) Safety Holdup: Any player about to execute a return who believes he is likely to strike an opponent with the ball or racquet may immediately stop play and request a dead-ball hinder. This call must be made immediately and is subject to acceptance and approval of the referee. The referee will grant a dead-ball hinder if he believes the holdup was reasonable and the player would have been able to return the shot. The referee may also determine to call an avoidable hinder if warranted.

7) Other Interference: Any other unintentional interference that prevents an opponent from having a fair chance to see or return the ball. Example: The ball obviously skids after striking a wet spot on the court floor or wall.

Rule 11B: Effect—A hinder call by the referee stops play and voids any situation following, such as the ball hitting a player. The only hinders a player may call are specified in Rules 11A.2, 11A.5 and 11A.6 and are subject to the acceptance of the referee. The effect of a dead-ball hinder is that the player who served will serve again, and will be awarded two serves.

Rule 11C: Avoidance:—While making an attempt to return the ball, a player is entitled to a fair chance to see and return the ball. It is the responsibility of the side that has just served or returned the ball to move so the receiving side may go straight to the ball and have an unobstructed view of the ball after it leaves the front wall. In the judgment of the referee, however, the receiver must make a reasonable effort to move toward the ball and have a reasonable chance to return the ball for a hinder to be called.

Rule 12: Avoidable Hinders (Point Hinder)—An avoidable hinder results in the loss of a rally.

An avoidable hinder does not necessarily have to be an intentional act and is a result of any of the following:

Rule 12A: Failure to Move—Player does not move sufficiently to allow an opponent a shot.

Rule 12B: Blocking—Player moves into a position effecting a block on the opponent about to return the ball, or in doubles, one partner moves in front of an opponent as the partner of that opponent is returning the ball.

Rule 12C: Moving into the Ball—Player moves in the way and is struck by the ball just played by the opponent.

Rule 12D: Pushing—Player deliberately pushes or shoves opponent during a rally.

Rule 12E: Restricts Opponent's Swing—Player moves, or fails to move, so as to restrict opponent's swing so the player returning the ball does not have a free, unimpeded swing.

Rule 12F: Intentional Distractions—Deliberate shouting, stamping of feet, waving of racquet, or any manner of disrupting the player who is hitting the ball.

Rule 12G: Wetting the Ball—Players, particularly the server, have the responsibility to see that the ball is kept dry at all times. Any ball wetting, deliberate or by accident, that is not corrected prior to the beginning of the rally, will result in an avoidable hinder.

Rule 13A: Rest-Period Timeouts—Each player or team is entitled to three 30-second timeouts in games to 15, and two 30-second timeouts in games to 11. Timeouts may not be called by either side after service motion has begun. Calling for a timeout when none remain or after service motion has begun, or taking more than 30 seconds in a timeout, will result in the assessment of a technical for delay of game.

Rule 13B: Injury Timeouts—If a player is injured during the course of a match as a result of contact with the ball, racquet, opponent, wall or floor, he will be granted an injury timeout. An injured player will not be allowed more than a total of 15 minutes of rest during the match. If the injured player is not able to resume play after total rest of 15 minutes, the match will be awarded to the opponent(s). Muscle cramps and pulls, fatigue, and other ailments not caused by direct contact on the court will not be considered an injury.

Rule 13C: Equipment Timeouts—Players are expected to keep all clothing and equipment in good, playable condition and are expected to use regular timeouts and time between games for adjustment and replacement of equipment. If a player or team is out of timeouts and the referee determines that an equipment change or adjustment is necessary for fair and safe continuation of the match, the referee may award an equipment timeout not to exceed two minutes.

Rule 13D: Timeouts Between Games—A five-minute rest period is allowed between all games of a match.

Rule 13E: Postponed Games—Any games postponed by referees will be resumed with the same score as when postponed.

Rule 14A: Technical Fouls—The referee is empowered to deduct one point from a player's or team's score when, in the referee's sole judgment, the player is being overtly and deliberately abusive. The actual invoking of this penalty is called a *referee's technical*. If after the technical is called against the abusing player, and the play is not immediately continued, the referee is empowered to forfeit the match in favor of the abusing player's opponent(s).

Some examples of actions that may result in technicals follow:

1) Profanity is an automatic technical and should be invoked by the referee whenever it occurs.

2) Excessive arguing.

3) Threat of any nature to opponent(s) or referee.

4) Excessive or hard striking of the ball between rallies.

5) Slamming of the racquet against walls or floor, slamming the door, or any action that might result in injury to the court or other player(s).

6) Delay of game, either in the form of taking too much time during timeouts and between games, in drying the court, in excessive questioning of the referee on the rules, or in excessive or unnecessary appeals.

7) International front-line foot faults to negate a bad lob serve.

8) Anything considered to be unsportsmanlike behavior.

Rule 14B: Technical Warning—If a player's behavior is not so severe as to warrant a referee's technical, a technical warning may be issued without point deduction.

Rule 14C: Effect—If a referee issues a technical warning, it will not result in a loss of rally or point and will be accompanied by a brief explanation of the reason for the warning. If a referee issues a referee's technical, one point will be removed from the offender's score. Awarding a technical will have no effect on service changes or sideouts. If the technical occurs either between games or when the offender has no points, the result will be that the offender's score will revert to −1.

IV HOW TO REFEREE WHEN THERE IS NO REFEREE

Rule 15: Safety—This is the primary and overriding responsibility of every player. At no time should the physical safety of players be compromised. Players are entitled, and expected, to hold up their swing, without penalty, any time they believe there might be a risk of physical contact. Any time a player says he held up to avoid contact, even if he was over-cautious, he is entitled to a hinder, a rally replayed without penalty.

Rule 16: Score—Because there is no referee or scorekeeper, it is important that there be no mis-understanding in this area. The server is required to announce both the server's and receiver's score before every first serve.

Rule 17: During Rallies—During rallies, it is generally the hitter's responsibility to make the call—if there is a possibility of a skip ball, double-bounce or illegal hit, play should continue until the hitter makes the call against himself. If the hitter does not make the call against himself and goes on to win the rally, and the player thought that none of the hitter's shots was good, he may appeal to the hitter by pointing out which shot he thought was bad and request the hitter to reconsider.

If the hitter is sure of his call and the opponent is still sure the hitter is wrong, the rally is replayed. As a matter of etiquette, players are expected to make calls against themselves any time they are not sure. In other words, if a shot is very close as to whether or not it was a good kill or a skip ball, unless the hitter is sure the shot was good, he should call it a skip.

Rule 18: Service—The following considerations apply:

1) Fault Serves (Long, Short, Ceiling and Three-Wall): The receiver has the primary responsibility to make these calls, and again, he should give the benefit of the doubt to his opponent whenever it is close. The receiver must make his call immediately, and not wait until he hits the ball and has the benefit of seeing how good a shot he can hit. It is not an option play—the receiver does not have the right to play a short serve just because he thinks that it is a setup.

2) Screen Serves: When there is no referee, a screen serve does not become an option play. When the receiver believes his view of the ball was sufficiently impaired to give the server too great an advantage on the serve, the receiver may hold up his swing and call a screen serve. Or, if he still feels he can make a good shot at the ball, he can say nothing and continue playing. He may not call a screen after he attempts to hit the ball.

Further, the server may not call a screen under any circumstance. He must simply expect to have to play the rally until he hears a call from the receiver. In doubles, unless the ball goes behind the back of the server's partner, no screens should be called.

3) Others: Foot faults, 10-second violations, receiving-line violations, service-zone